VANESSA SIEMENS

50 States of Grief

Copyright © 2025 by Vanessa Siemens

All rights reserved. No part of this publication may be reproduced, stored or transmitted in any form or by any means, electronic, mechanical, photocopying, recording, scanning, or otherwise without written permission from the publisher. It is illegal to copy this book, post it to a website, or distribute it by any other means without permission.

First edition

This book was professionally typeset on Reedsy.
Find out more at reedsy.com

For Mom
Thank you for loving me so completely and teaching me how to live with tenderness, confidence, courage, and faith. Your absence is felt daily, but your life continues to shape me. This book wouldn't exist without you. I love you, always.

For Parks, Paisley, Stormi, Starlow, Mila, Aiden, and Whitney
You are my joys, my reminders of what matters most. Thank you for teaching me to keep choosing love, silliness, and life—even in the middle of grief. Keep shining your light.

Contents

II Essays on Grief

Introduction

Grief has become my lifelong companion. Once an unwelcome, unwanted stranger, it is now a friend who invites me to experience the beauty and richness of life. As a child, I grieved freely about the little things, like needing to get out of the pool and go home, to the bigger things, like my parents' divorce. As I grew up, I slammed the door in grief's face. I started to ignore and deny that there was grief that needed to be felt. I didn't want to experience the pain it caused. I didn't understand how to grieve while trusting in a loving and good God. I forged ahead, attempting to leave grief behind, not realizing I was also leaving a piece of myself behind.

The crux of this book is a story of a road trip of grief. It was a pilgrimage of sorts. Of course, pilgrimages usually involve walking, but I chose to drive instead. I decided to title my pilgrimage, '50 States of Grief' and set out to travel across all 50 states of the USA between April and August of 2017. I wanted to mark a transition in my life out of a season of grieving, into a season of life and wholeness, and I wanted to write about it. The ignorance and fear of grief I experienced in my early years caused a lot of harm later in my life, and I wanted to share my experiences with others who have felt similarly at times. Although my trip didn't move me out of a season of grieving as I had originally expected, it became a giant step in moving through a more intense season of mourning and taught me how to live with grief as my lifelong companion.

My mom had died a year and a half before my road trip. While I was her caregiver, I told her that I would be going on this trip after she died. She loved the idea, not only that I would take time to grieve, but especially that I would do it through an activity we both loved.

My mom and I used to travel together… a LOT. Every year (or sometimes twice a year) we would embark on a mother-daughter trip. The impetus for our trips was usually a conversation like this:

Me: Hey Mom, we should go to ________ (usually this was a very random place)

Mom: Fun! I've always wanted to go there. When are we going?

A few days later…

Mom: Did you book the trip yet?

Me: Oh, I was just joking, I didn't think we would actually go. But if you are serious, let's definitely go.

Within a couple months we were usually on our way to a new destination around the world. We had about ten years of travelling adventures and went to countless countries. While it seemed a bit excessive at the time, little did we know when planning these trips that my mom's time on earth would be cut short and I would be left with deep gratitude for our crazy travels, and hold each memory dear. I am thankful that we said yes to those whims and embraced spontaneity in heading off to the next destination.

My mom found out she had stage four cancer in June 2013. I was living in Quebec at the time. I had sold everything and moved across the country and had planned on staying in Quebec long term. I was developing a community of deep friendships and had no plans to return to BC. When I heard the news, I moved home as soon as I could, to serve as her primary caregiver. Cancer wasn't new for my mom. At 17, against all odds, my mom had survived stage four Hodgkin's. She'd always been a fighter, and I think this made her lung cancer seem surreal. She was a survivor. She would beat this. When I arrived home, my mom's health was going rapidly downhill and it looked like she would die within a few months. Amazingly, she ended up living for another two and a half years. At the time, that reality seemed impossible.

Before my mom got sick, I thought we had become immune to loss (at least for the next while). My family was well acquainted with loss. When I was eight, shortly after my grandpa died (with whom I had a really special relationship), my parents were divorced, changing the dynamic of the family from that moment forward. When I was 16, my oldest brother, Leon died in a motorbike accident at 20 years of age. My dad died a year and a half later from a heart attack and both of his parents, my grandparents, died within nine months of him. As I said, my family knew grief. We were finally in a season where life seemed stable again. My mom was enjoying being a grandma. We were in a good rhythm of travel and had a dear friendship. It felt like we were untouchable. Life wasn't steeped in heartache and loss. Or so we thought.

To say the fall of 2013 was hard is an understatement. Suddenly my relationship with my mom was inverted. I slept on the floor next to her hospital bed in the living room, so I could help her in the middle of the night if necessary. I was thrown into a new world of managing someone else's pain, administering drugs, and trying to make my mom as comfortable as possible in the midst of navigating my deepest fears of losing her, while watching her change and weaken before me.

My mom did get better for a little while. Although she was still sick and couldn't do everything she did before, we had a chance to travel together as a family and celebrate life in different ways. Our first "final" family trip was to Great Wolf Lodge, south of Seattle. Since my mom was feeling better with time, we went on our second final family trip to Disneyland. Our third, and actual, final family trip was to Hawaii. My mom and I also went on a final mother-daughter trip to Portland and the Oregon Coast, where I was able to show her where I was going to school and take her to some of my favourite places. We were grateful for time at home together and time spent travelling.

We had the opportunity to say good-bye over the next two years. It was a strange season of waiting and living. The tug-of-war between trips to the hospital and glimpses of "regular life" threatened to tear me in two. It was still unreal to fathom life without my mom. I assumed our new normal would continue indefinitely, so I clung to the hope of her complete healing, unable to imagine life without her. I wondered if (and desperately hoped) this would be a short season of illness. We would look back on these difficult times and see how it served to form and strengthen us for the future, bringing us closer together in the process.

There were many doctor visits filled with great hope. A few tumours were shrinking or hadn't grown, however, tests revealed that there were new spots showing up in her body and reality started settling in that maybe the cancer wouldn't completely disappear this time.

Although my mom and I were close, we weren't always the best at having hard conversations. As I journeyed with her though, we would find ways to talk about her up-coming death and what life might look like after. My mom loved the idea of me going on a grieving trip. My original plan was to go to Portugal and Spain as that was our next planned mother-daughter destination. Everything started coming together for a road trip through the United States and it felt like the right journey to take.

This book is not a theological treatise on grief. It is my shared experience from what I have walked, a reflection of my personal journey. Writing a book has been beyond exciting for me while equally scaring the shit out of me. It's scary to put down my experience and thoughts in words. What if they change? I want to extend grace for this, because we are constantly growing and changing and we are transient. I have gone through many seasons of grief in my life, but by no means does that make me an expert. I have learned some deep truths along the way. My road trip helped solidify and bring meaning to much of my journey. Now I want to share some of my journey with others. I can only share from my experiences, and I recognize they might be vastly different from what the next person has walked through.

The older I become, the more I realize that life is a series of losses that must be grieved. However, it is also filled with gifts. Life is a myriad of losses and gifts. I find we tend to focus on the gift part and neglect to process the pain and hurt from the loss. At different points in life, I have struggled to find spaces able to hold me in my grief. So, I want to share my story, told through the lens of my 50 states road trip (Part 1) and some essays I wrote on grief (Part 2). My hope is that my story might speak to you wherever you are on your journey. May this book provide a familiar space for your grief. There is no expectation for how you should be or what your grief should look like. If it looks different from mine, that's okay. Regardless, I hope you walk away feeling seen and encouraged.

I

50 States of Grief—The Road Trip

1

Washington

Goosebumps formed on my arms as I got out of the car. The fresh air tickled my nostrils as it carried the smell of beauty. The tulips were an explosion of colours. I was seeing the red of my mom's lipstick, the yellow of her sundress, the purple of that scarf she used to wear. The wind carried a cacophony of tumult and silence. I could taste the dirt of the fields. The wind filled my senses while leaving me deflated in the same breath.

I had been here before, but never alone.

I walk through the tulip fields, pausing at each row, feeling a roller coaster of sadness and happiness as memories flood my mind. My mom used to love coming to see the tulips in La Connor. We used to walk down this path in the spring.

I'm at the beginning of this "grieving road trip", and am surprised that tulip fields are triggering my grief in ways I had not anticipated. Building up to this "grieving road trip", a lot of people told me it would be hard and they commended me for creating this space in my life for grief. I brushed their comments aside. I had spent the last two years grieving and this trip would be a transition to a season of not grieving. It would be closure and moving into acceptance. The lump in my throat as I walked through the tulip fields told me otherwise.

Grief isn't merely a season. It lacks predictability and doesn't conform to our timelines. It can be triggered in the most unexpected (and inconvenient) moments. It is that moment while driving and happily singing a song that morphs into sobbing. It is the delight of blooming tulips intertwined with the sadness of not being able to share it with my mom. It is driving down the I-5 in Washington, excited about my road trip, while simultaneously remembering all the times my mom and I drove down this road. It is the sweetness of past memories and the devastation of not being able to create future memories with her.

Travelling reminds me so deeply of my mom. There was a time right after she died that I told myself I never wanted to travel again. This was a crazy declaration. Those who know me would laugh at the impossibility of this notion. However, in the moment, it felt too difficult. I didn't want to be reminded that she wasn't there to share it with me. For the two and a half years after her diagnosis, and for about a year after she died, I stayed home and didn't venture out much. I felt raw and broken and didn't know if I would be able to enjoy travelling as I once had. And yet here I am, venturing on this trip and it begins with me being bombarded with grief and the pain of loss.

As I left the tulip fields and drove down the I-5 through Washington, I started to notice the trees. The winter in BC that year had been long and all our trees were still without leaves. The further I drove, the more green and lush the landscape around me became. Suddenly I was surrounded by new life, bursting in its vibrancy of colour, ushering me into my journey toward deeper grieving and healing. As the trees passed, hope welled up within. Loss and pain are very real, but so is the promise of restoration and healing. Here I am, embarking on important steps of that journey. Each kilometre I drive builds the anticipation and joy of what is to come, along with the reassurance that facing and walking through the pain of loss is worth it.

2

Oregon

Seriously, God? Water pelted my face and I could no longer differentiate my tears from the rain. Dragging the garbage toward the road in the pouring rain, it felt heavy and hard. We talked to the doctor today and it doesn't look good. The cancer in my mom's brain has spread and among other complications, the next few months will likely include loss of eyesight, shifts in personality, and pain. So much pain.

It's too much for me, God. I can't watch her suffer anymore. After everything she has been through, it's going to get worse? I can't stand to see her in pain, but I can't let her go. Why haven't you healed her yet? The burden of what's ahead feels too heavy, too impossible. If you won't heal her, can you make the road ahead less harsh? I'm not ready to say goodbye, but I also can't bear to lose more of her while she's alive.

Every part of me is drenched as I relinquish the final bag of garbage beside the road. Feeling lighter as I walk back to the house, I no longer notice the rain through my torrent of tears.

"You look cold."

It's raining and the torrent of Multnomah Falls almost drowns out the stranger's voice, which jolts me from my flashback. Remembering where I am, and being launched back into the present moment, I look up and smile, hoping my tears are mistaken for rain on my face.

Laughing, I respond, "A rain jacket would have been handy." Looking down at my flip flops, "I guess shoes would have also been a good idea." The stranger smiles back as they walk down the path and I continue upward. My thoughts turn back to the memory that had been interrupted. When I dragged the garbage to the road, I didn't know my mom would die a week later. I wrestled with God, "Will you heal her, God, or will she just suffer even more before she dies?" I didn't get an answer right then, but the rain soaking me mirrored the presence of God enveloping me in a moment and season when I felt alone and broken. Each drop of rain was a reminder that God was near and wept with me.

Dragging the garbage to the road that night was a significant moment of encountering God. My experience of encountering God at Multnomah Falls and feeling God's presence and healing in my grief as I revisited hard memories, has now been added to my list of such moments. Waterfalls are mesmerizing—watching the water tumble over the side and crash into the water below never fails to inspire awe and wonder. I sat there, soaked with the presence of God, knowing I would be okay. Amid all the remaining unanswered questions, I wasn't alone and there was hope for the road ahead.

3

Idaho

When all you expect are potatoes, it's not hard to exceed expectations. My time in Idaho was short, yet exceeded my expectations. I didn't even see any potatoes—I guess technically my expectations weren't met at all, but it was so much better. I had pictured flat potato fields that go on for miles. The Idaho license plate, "Scenic Idaho" should have been a dead giveaway that my expectations were quite misguided. There are mountains, cities, breathtaking rivers that snake through the landscape, miles of interesting clouds, picturesque abandoned houses, and fields (with things other than potatoes).

Most of my life has been far different from my expectations:

- I didn't expect my parents to divorce when I was younger.
- I expected to become a horse-riding acrobat when I grew up.
- I didn't expect my oldest brother, Leon, to die unexpectedly at the young age of 20.
- I expected to graduate university with a degree in math.
- I didn't expect to still be single.
- I expected to have children and a family of my own.
- I didn't expect my dad to die when I was 18.
- I expected to live in Quebec long-term after moving there.
- I didn't expect my mom to get cancer.

- I expected that my mom would be healed.
- I didn't expect to be her caregiver for two years, walking alongside her until she died.
- I expected grief would be easier to navigate after having grieved in the past.
- I didn't expect depression.
- I didn't expect the weariness of grief.
- I didn't expect the mixture of unpredictable emotions.

My list of expectations, and I suspect yours as well, is very long. We build expectations and hopes for what life will hold and these expectations are often disappointed. Sometimes life feels cruel. Life is painful and hard at times.

I could focus on where my expectations were not met, but when I look back, life has also exceeded so many of my expectations:

- I didn't expect to have such a rich tapestry of friendships.
- I expected to be stuck in a job I didn't love.
- I didn't expect to travel the world.
- I expected to study math only because I was good at it.
- I didn't expect to have so many unique life opportunities.
- I expected to be alone for holidays.
- I didn't expect to study psychology and spiritual formation.
- I expected to stay exactly as I always had been.
- I didn't expect the depth of joy that grief carved out.

Sometimes I get caught up on the expectations that have led to disappointment. I focus on the hard things. At other times, we keep our expectations low and yet life comes along and blows those expectations away by greatly exceeding them. Life is beautiful. Life is infused with hope. Life is joy-giving and vibrant.

It's important to pay attention to our expectations. Part of grief is recognizing the sadness where expectations haven't been met. The other side of that is those parts of life that unexpectedly surprise and delight us and need to be celebrated. We must grieve. But we also must celebrate.

I could fixate on where life hasn't measured up to my expectations or I can take it for what it is and find beauty and delight that is also muddled throughout life. I could have driven through Idaho searching for potato fields and been upset that it didn't meet my expectations. Instead, I had the chance to delight in the beauty around me, to celebrate, and allow myself to be fully present to each moment rather than distracted by a vain search for potato fields.

4

California

California welcomed me with torrential downpours. "Welcome to sunny California"—ha. It also provided fog so thick I could barely see the vehicle in front of me. I took an exit to grab a coffee and drove by Starbucks three times because I couldn't actually see it through the fog. I finally turned into the driveway that the signs seemed to be pointing to, trusting that the Starbucks would be there, and it was. I couldn't see it from the road but had to blindly turn into a parking lot to find it.

Fog has become a theme in my life that won't go away. Fog first became a prominent image in my life in the difficult season of being a caregiver for my mom. During some respite time, I was able to go on a couple road trips. I had mapped out my destinations and picked some of my favourite places to visit. I was highly anticipating taking lots of great pictures. I would be driving on a beautiful sunny day and the moment I turned on a road leading to the ocean, the car would be surrounded by fog. The closer I got to my destination, the foggier it became. Disappointment was my initial response because the coast is breathtaking on a sunny day, however, as I started taking pictures and playing with the settings on my camera, I realized that foggy scenes are just as beautiful in a completely different way.

Fog adds an element of mystery and wonder. You know there is something beautiful and majestic in sight, and yet you can only catch a glimpse of that beauty. These glimpses create an internal desire to find and see more beauty and delight. Yet each step you take, new things become revealed to you. As you enter the fog, you are given a new way of seeing things. Even though the fog limited my view, I was able to see something extra on those foggy days. I was able to see beauty in the unexpected. One of my newfound favourite moments is when light shines through fog. Fog spreads sunlight in new ways - a symbol of hope and life in the midst of bleakness.

Grief has felt like living in fog. The way ahead is obscured, offering only glimpses. It doesn't make sense. It is disorienting. It can be damp, grey and depressing and yet it holds beauty and mystery. It offers an invitation to step forward, choosing to trust that God goes before me when the way ahead seems impossible.

Grief is riddled with obscurity. It is impossible to juggle all the thoughts and emotions that arise. My view of God and life is challenged. And yet as I step into grief and all that it brings, it helps me see a bit more clearly. As I trust God in the path God has laid before me, my trust goes deeper. When the disappointment and confusion consume me like a shroud of fog, I choose to look for the unique beauty it brings.

The rain and fog welcoming me to California feels like an invitation to remember these truths. Fog is often part of the journey. Growing up, my family travelled to California frequently, but this time was an opportunity to visit friends in places I had never been. Many of the friends I'm staying with on this journey are people I went to seminary with. These are people who walked through the fog with me and encouraged me to continue taking steps forward into the fog.

Fog is my continual reminder to notice beauty in the unexpected. It is an invitation to take the next step.

5

Nevada

I drove through Nevada twice. The first was when I left Idaho for California. The second was on my way from California to Utah.

Both drives were beautiful for different reasons. During the first one, it was pouring rain for most of it, but the mountains were shrouded in fog and felt full of mystery and intrigue. There were long dirt roads that stretched through the fields leading toward the mountains. Then I ended up in Reno—what a gorgeous backdrop for a city. I'm not a big city fan, but being surrounded by majestic snow-capped mountains makes a city more stunning. The drive through the mountains through piles of snow was breathtaking but also very windy. My door almost flew off each time I got out to take pictures and walk around.

My second drive was quite the opposite. It was extremely hot. This resulted in a very lopsided burn. I learned that putting on expired sunscreen at the end of the day doesn't retroactively stop you from getting a burn. I also learned that opening a map and trying to refold it while driving a convertible is a fruitless activity. The day of driving felt more light-hearted and fun with moments to laugh at myself and the antics of driving alone for long stretches. I passed Las Vegas on my way through and once again was awed at such a beautiful setting for this city.

I didn't do anything overly spectacular in Nevada. And yet I enjoyed it just as much as some of the other places I've visited. It was beautiful with a mix of crazy weather to be enjoyed. I tried to take in each moment as it came.

Sometimes I focus too much on the spectacular and extraordinary. I deem things or experiences valuable when they end with deep insights or 'aha' moments. I count things as worthy depending on my level of engagement. While the spectacular is wonderful, unfortunately it also means I often miss out on the extraordinary that is found in the ordinary. Like the extraordinary that is found on a rainy farm highway going through Nevada. Or the extraordinary beauty found on a rainy day when you can't see half the landscape. Or the extraordinary growth and life found in the midst of a desert. Or the extraordinary humour found in conversations with oneself while driving. Yet as I slowed down and took notice, just driving through Nevada was spectacular.

I am learning to trust that each moment is significant. As I am present to each moment, no matter how it measures up to my expectations or how grand it may or may not have been, there is an invitation to see the extraordinary within that moment. Beyond being externally significant, each moment has internal significance, both in personal growth and transformation. I trust that God is continually doing work within me as I am present to God, myself and the world around me wherever I am currently placed. How amazing that every moment is made extraordinary as I am aware of God's presence with me. I am able to receive the gift of engaging fully moment by moment.

Of course, finding the extraordinary in the ordinary isn't a struggle when life is full of good things and happy moments. I suspect, and have found it to be true, that this applies to painful moments as well. Each moment is an opportunity to receive grace from God's fullness. This thought baffles me every time I try to wrap my mind around it. From God's fullness we have received grace upon grace, endless and spectacular. God is meeting me in my moments of sorrow. There is an abundance of grace. How extraordinary.

There have been moments in times of intense grief where all I can do is be present. It is tempting in those moments to occupy my mind with a brain-numbing activity, or to distract myself with humour. But sometimes an extraordinary and mysterious type of healing takes place in those moments when we stop and are present with our grief, allowing ourselves to sit with it, notice it and to feel it. The significance of sitting with grief in a moment may not be evident at first, but over time, I suspect the healing results of pausing to be with grief will have deep impact. Sometimes just being present is as much spectacular involvement as you need.

6

Utah

"Grace is the beginning of our healing because it offers the one thing we need most: to be accepted without regard to whether we are acceptable. Grace stands for gift; it is the gift of being accepted before we become acceptable." - Lewis Smedes, Shame and Grace

Utah wins for being the most underrated and surprising state.

From the moment I crossed the border into Utah, I was taken back by the incredible beauty. Every ten minutes I found myself pulling over to take pictures.

My first stop was Zion National Park. Wow. The drive up to the park itself is beautiful because you can see the mountains in the distance as you approach. I was able to stay for sunset. There were endless breathtaking views and around each corner was a sight that was grand and awe-inspiring. My words and pictures will never be able to do it justice. There were lots of places to pull over and take it all in and various trail heads to meander on.

Next was Bryce Canyon National Park. Whereas I could see Zion from afar, with Bryce, all I could see was a bunch of trees. It is a canyon after all. On the way there you are questioning whether there is in fact a canyon because the landscape leads you to think otherwise. En route, I drove through Red Canyon which lit up like flames as the sun was setting, building my anticipation for what Bryce Canyon would be like.

The next morning I was up early and decided to watch the sunrise over the canyon. I kept going to different viewpoints and it felt more and more surreal because it was so breathtaking. It was fairly cold and there was still snow in some places, but it felt like I had the park to myself.

As the day warmed, more people showed up. I love talking to strangers and enjoyed chatting with a couple from Kentucky who gave me some suggestions of places to go and offered to meet up with me in Kentucky. I appreciate random connections with people. In fact, some of the people I'm visiting on this trip are the result of befriending strangers.

I went back to my hotel to nap. I felt guilty, because here I was in such a beautiful place and I should be exploring it 24/7. Nonetheless, it was a glorious three hour nap and I realized I could have time to rest and still enjoy the park. That afternoon I enjoyed a three hour hike, drove to Red Canyon for another sunset and returned to Bryce to stargaze. There was a lot packed into the day even though I took a few hours for rest. "Past Vanessa" would have pushed herself, been exhausted and suffered for it as a result. I'm learning to have grace with myself and to recognize that it's okay not to do everything. Sometimes doing "nothing" is necessary for our well being. I didn't feel like I missed out on anything but likely enjoyed the day more because I rested. My rest enabled me to be more present and take it all in more deeply.

Every year, I pick a word, and my word for that year was grace. It flows from years of being too hard on myself and pushing myself too much. There are many facets to grace, from God extending grace to us and us being able to extend grace to ourselves and those around us. I am quick to extend grace to others while holding it back from myself. Maybe you've experienced this too. My three months of travelling around the US is an extension of grace to myself, creating space to continue to grieve and process, but also to continue engaging life in whatever capacity I'm able to in the midst of grief.

Through this grieving journey, grace has been crucial. Grief has a habit of rearing its head at the most inopportune moments and I don't always stop to listen to it or to myself. I don't always allow myself space to notice it and tend to it. I shove it back down and continue with whatever lies before me.

Grace invites me to create space, even if it's just a few moments to grieve, and even in the moments where I don't feel like grief should be rising up. Grief cannot be controlled, nor should I judge myself if it appears in inconvenient situations.

Grace was found again as I hiked back out of Bryce Canyon. The way down is beautiful but also accompanied with the knowledge that I have to hike back out of the canyon. I had no agenda and was able to stop to catch my breath and not feel bad about it. I loved being able to take in more of the gorgeous views and would have repeated encounters with people I met on the walk back out:

Random Stranger: Hello again. Isn't this so stunning? See you at the next stop!

Me: *smiles and laughs because I'm too out of breath to respond.*

I'm so thankful for grace. The more I learn about it and experience it, the more I realize how multi-faceted and broad it is. From God's fullness we have received grace upon grace. Do we actually allow ourselves to receive it?

7

Arizona

"The soul is like a wild animal...tough, resilient, resourceful, savvy, and self-sufficient: it knows how to survive in hard places. Yet despite its toughness, the soul is also shy. Just like a wild animal, it seeks safety in the dense underbrush, especially when other people are around. If we want to see a wild animal, we know that the last thing we should do is go crashing through the woods yelling for it to come out. But if we will walk quietly into the woods, sit patiently at the base of a tree...the wild creature we seek might put in an appearance."
- *Parker Palmer, A Hidden Wholeness*

I keep expecting to be disappointed. I woke up this morning, feeling saturated and slightly exhausted from all my experiences. This is only the beginning. There's much to come—can I keep up like this for another two months?

I'm still blown away by the beauty I've seen. There has been so much wonder stirred up within me. I have been able to be present to each moment in a way I haven't experienced before. In each moment I wonder how anything can compare to what I have just seen. And yet at the next moment, I am taken aback once again. And yet, I feel this weight within. Grief has been trickling out in different ways and yet it needs more of my attention. Although this is my grieving road trip, I have allowed it to help me ignore my grief. In fact, I think part of me had secretly hoped to ditch grief somewhere along the way, and move on with life, unburdened and free. As I travel, my mom's memory is tucked in close. The weight of loss that accompanies that memory is heavy and deep. I don't want to look at those emotions right now. I just want to drive and enjoy the landscape.

I lug my bags to my car and look up at the disappearing night sky. It is early and the world around me still sleeps. Turning on my headlights, the gravel crunches as I leave the parking lot and follow the map to Arizona.

Left. Right. Left. Right. I don't know where to look anymore because the landscape is stunning and I can't soak it all in. I catch glimpses of rivers that have carved canyons out of the rocks. I see wild desert flowers on the side of the road. The red in the mountains is a deep and beautiful colour. The rest stop—oh shoot, I should stop there. There's a shoulder ahead I can turn around on. I feel my leg muscles as I get out of my car. It might be a good idea to stop more frequently to stretch my legs.

My hand rises to turn the vehicle on, but I decide to quickly check my phone. The email I have been anticipating is waiting for me in my inbox. My heart beating faster, I read the email and am crestfallen. In one email, my carefully laid out plans for the fall are ruined. Seriously, God? Can't anything go right for me? I thought this was your plan. Now I'm faced with no plans. Being a caregiver for my mom consumed over two years of my life. Now I have an empty slate again with no idea how to fill it. This was my plan.

I turn the key, and jerk the steering wheel, speeding out of the parking lot. Biting my lip, I drive with determination. I stare ahead, ignoring the tears that are welling up. Is life simply one disappointment after another? The moment I take a step forward, I'm shoved two steps back. God, what in the world are you up to? This doesn't make sense and I'm tired of having my plans laid to waste. Argh. Silence fills my vehicle as I continue driving. My grunts of frustration pierce the silence.

I'm surrounded by beautiful landscape but I don't want to enjoy it because I'm angry. That area is beautiful, but God, I feel hurt. I feel invisible, unseen. Do you even care about me? Tears roll down my cheek and my hand swipes them away. Anger is easier. On my left, I pass a parking lot. What's over there that's worth stopping for? I keep driving but my curiosity makes me do a u-turn. I park. It's hot out. Whatever. I will take a picture and keep going.

Walking through the sandy parking lot, I stop at the fence to take a picture. Wait, there's a path that leads between the hills. My feet propel me forward. Oh good, I'm trudging through a sandy, dried up riverbed. Sand sneaks into my flip flops, so hot it burns my feet as I walk. I kick the sand. Sweat snakes down my back, soaking my dress. Why in the world am I walking in the desert in flip flops and a dress? I don't even care what's here. Walking in sand sucks. This was a dumb idea.

I continue kicking the sand, my anger now directed toward the sand and the heat. God, why did you create this? Here I am walking in misery. This is horrible.

Step by step, my anger dissolves as my layers are peeled back, revealing deeper places of hurt and disappointment with God. I'm disappointed about my failed plans for the fall, yes. But deeper than that I am hurt and devastated that God took my mom. God already took my brother and my dad and my grandparents. It feels like too much. I'm an orphan at 30. I don't have my own family. I'm alone. Why me? Why now? Are you there God? Do you care? Do you see me? You're God, you're perfect. In the face of this truth, can I be disappointed and hurt? This is my honest expression of how I feel because I don't understand life. I don't understand pain and loss and its seemingly random distribution.

Looking down, I see a desert flower. In the midst of barrenness, life and beauty has fought for a place to grow and exist. Through the tears I offer a smile at this reflection of God's character. Hope. Life. I keep trudging up the river bank and turn a final corner where piles of rocks are gathered. It has a unique beauty. God created all of this. This riverbed holds history. It is dried up and yet it has created a stunning landscape. God, I am hurt and sad, but you are good. Your goodness is reflected around me. And you have been faithful.

In the midst of the barrenness of the desert, I feel God's voice, "You can trust me." I can trust you. I don't understand. And I'm still sad. I need to cling to this because the weight of sadness and disappointment is strong.

I return to my car, feeling a bit lighter. Tears accompany me as I pour my heart out while driving. God is present - I can feel it. God sees me. God hears me. This knowledge is a balm to my wounded heart. I still feel sad and disappointed, but not without hope.

After a lengthy drive, and counting down the miles to Page, Arizona, I see it as a speck on the distant horizon. Wait, is that a lake? There's a gigantic lake. It's beautiful. And unexpected. Lake Powell. I follow the sign to a parking lot. It looks like a long walk. It is. It's still hot but as I walk toward the lake, I feel a deep sense of peace within. It is beautiful. There is a giant rock in the middle. There are desert flowers scattered around. I sit down and take it in. The water is so blue. There is a slight breeze. I can't even see where the lake ends. God is so big. I am small. I can trust God. I don't want to leave but my exhaustion is inviting me to rest at my hotel in Page.

* * *

My first stop the next morning is Horseshoe Bend. My breath is taken away as I catch the first glimpse of the river as it loops around. My speed quickens as I go down the hill. I walk to the edge. There are no railings. Be careful. I peek over to see the cliff. It is a dizzying feeling to glance over and realize that with a nudge I could easily be knocked over. I snap a picture. And another picture. I can barely fit the entire scene into my camera. I take some more pictures. Vanessa, stop taking pictures, you have about 50 of the same thing. I can't capture it. It's too big. It's too beautiful. Could God be this good? Could I trust God?

I could stare at this forever but I don't want to be late for my Antelope Canyon tour. I'm so excited. I've been waiting years to visit Antelope Canyon. I check in and wait. We load up on the trucks and the drive feels unsteady, like we will tip over at any moment, but we finally arrive. The jeep parks outside a small entrance into the rocks. I'm thankful it hasn't rained in the last couple days. This is the desert so the slightest amount of rain, even far away, can flood the canyon in an instant, which is why tours are required. We follow our guide and instantly my ears are filled with the gasps of the others, soon joined by my own. Wow. The red rock is covered in swirls. I look up. The bright blue sky against the red is beautiful. I touch the wall. It's cold and smooth. I run my hand along the rock, feeling connected to all the people who have walked through here before me. My group is getting ahead. I follow quickly. The guide is telling stories.

"See that debris up there? That is from a recent flood. That's how high the water gets."

I crane my neck. Really? Images of water filling the canyon enter my mind, a testament to the destructive power of water. Much of what I've been seeing was carved by water. As people prattle around me, awe fills me with silence.

We pile again into the back of the truck, and I begin chatting with some ladies,

"Wasn't that amazing?"

"Yes, it is hard to take it all in. Where are you ladies from?"

"We're from Colorado. We are on a spiritual journey, travelling to different places of healing. Our next stop is Sedona. I couldn't stop touching the walls, I felt a deeper power here."

We continued our conversation, sharing our stories and journeys toward healing. Although we used different language to describe it, they felt what I had felt. I treasured those moments of feeling God's presence and power reflected in God's creation. God is big, and worthy of my trust.

* * *

After an overnight stay in Page, I set out early in the morning for the Grand Canyon. I was anxious to get there as a lifetime of hearing about it was waiting to put an image to the words. Pulling into the parking lot, there are butterflies in my stomach. This feels surreal. I am picturing dirt paths and rustic areas. This is a giant parking lot. The visitor's centre is huge. I walk past it and am confronted with crowds of people. I see past them. The canyon opens up before me. It's breathtaking. The crowds vie for my attention as they scramble to get to the edge of the viewing area. Dozens of selfie sticks mar the horizon as tourists try to get the perfect Grand Canyon selfie. I'm going to keep walking.

The farther I walk, the less crowded it is. There's the perfect spot. There are barely any people around. There's a big rock to sit on. I sit in stillness and silence, letting all my thoughts and emotions and anguish from the past days settle. Breathe in. Breathe out. I breathe in the serenity of the moment, taking in the vast landscape before me.

Breathing deep, in, out, in, out. Suddenly a bug lands on my arm. There are bugs all around. There are butterflies fluttering. I hear birdsong around me, as birds fly around me, diving into the canyon. I hear and feel the breeze. Suddenly a squirrel pops up and comes toward me, an uninvited guest. Life becomes present all around me. Things I had not noticed in the crowds or while walking. By stopping I could become still. In the midst of my noticing, I could sense God's presence with me. God is with me. I can trust God.

After a long time of sitting and taking it all in, I get up and return to my car. Heading toward New Mexico, I reflect on my time in Arizona. It was filled with expressions of hurt and disappointment. In the midst of being surrounded by stunning places, I was also filled with anguish. The places I visited became safe spaces for me to express my feelings to God and to lament. Over and over again, God was reminding me of God's goodness and faithfulness. God is bigger than my finite mind can understand. I can trust Divine Love. I can be honest with how I feel. I can trust that God is healing me in deep places I cannot see. In these moments when I resist restlessness, forcing myself to stop, to be still and know that God is God, these become places of healing. These are places where I allow myself to surrender and trust. In the moments where I don't understand what is happening, I can trust. In the moments where the whys bring deep anguish, I can trust. Amid my swirling emotions, I can trust. God is present in all of it and I can trust God in and through it all.

Each "why" becomes an invitation from God for an encounter. I can ask my questions and recognize they likely won't be answered. I can seek to know more of who God is so I can continue trusting in the midst of not understanding the bigger picture. The truths about who God is doesn't invalidate my emotions, but rather they give me the freedom to hold the tension of the two together.

8

New Mexico

When I was born, my mom wanted to name me Sasha Renee. My dad insisted on Vanessa and my mom chose Maree for my middle name (partly named after her, Marie, and partly keeping the two e's from her initial pick). The Greek meaning for Vanessa is butterfly. Befittingly, my life journey has encompassed the life cycle of a butterfly. The butterfly has become symbolic in my life for transformation through loss, much like a caterpillar who after metamorphosis, leaves behind the cocoon to enter a new and glorious stage of life as a butterfly. I love my name and it holds a great depth of meaning for me.

Names are important. They tell a story. They are informative. They contain history. They give dignity to what is named. Even the name 'New Mexico' at first glance, speaks to its history. While looking at the map of New Mexico, I saw multiple place names and wondered how the name would manifest itself in each town. My imagination can run wild in imagining different scenarios of how a name came to be.

Red Hill. Twin Arrows. Two Guns. Pie Town. I hoped Pie Town would be true to its name. The next day I set out with a keen eye to see what these towns would be like. In Red Hill, there was a big red hill. In Twin Arrows, there were two giant arrow monuments. In Two Guns… well, I didn't actually look into that one.

And then I entered Pie Town. The multiple signs advertising pie shops assured me that it was aptly named. The name tells a bit of its history and it drew me in to learn more about this town that came to be due to home made pies. A man named Clyde Norman opened a bakery in the 1920's called Pie Town and although the town is similar to a ghost town now, they have multiple pie shops and an annual pie festival. I enjoyed some pie at 'Pie-O-neer' and learned more from the ladies working there.

Throughout New Mexico, I was again surprised at some of the beautiful landscapes. At this point I had been by myself for a few days (and may have been at the point where one feels slightly crazed) and decided to play 'Hey Cow' while driving. The way you play is by yelling "Hey Cow!" when you pass cows and you get points for however many cows turn their heads to look at you. In the absence of having anyone to play with, I decided a healthy competition would be struck between the left and right side of my vehicle. The left side won 10-0. Lest you think that cows on the left side of my vehicle were more responsive, I will disclose that I only saw about 10 cows. Needless to say, it was great entertainment for ten minutes of my drive. Although my game was silly and fun, I was struck with the thought that even cows know their names and respond when called (or they respond to crazy people driving by and yelling out the window, but for the purposes of this story, let's just pretend that's not the case).

Two other spectacular spots in New Mexico were White Sands National Monument and Carlsbad Caverns National Park, both appropriately named for what you would expect to see. At White Sands, there were endless white sand dunes contrasting against the mountains in the background. Carlsbad Caverns was a massive cave you can walk into and after the walk, there was a spot to sit and watch hundreds of bats fly out at dusk.

Being in all these places reminded me of a quote from Gregory of Nazianzus, a 4th century theologian. He talks about Jesus assuming our humanity and is known for saying, "What has not been assumed has not been healed." Jesus had to become flesh to heal us. It is a thought that has stuck with me and as I journey, I have connected it to names.

I have learned that in most situations, what has not been named cannot be healed. Much of my life has been full of pain. I have felt the pain in my gut, I have felt its weight and burden and have often felt paralyzed by it. Picture a million different threads that are all knotted and tangled together to form a giant ball. This giant ball has been a symbol for my pain as I have allowed it to build up.

Through my journey of grieving, I have learned the importance of naming the different threads. The importance of untangling it, and pulling threads out so I can see them for what they are. This allows me to name each one and bring it before God to be healed. The naming might involve identifying a specific emotion that is evoked within. Simply calling it 'pain' doesn't actually let me understand or let go of it. The naming also might involve a specific event or situation that I need to bring before God to heal and redeem.

As I pull out each thread, the ball becomes smaller. I am able to let go and I feel less stuck and jumbled. As I name different emotions, I can allow myself to feel them and move on. Pulling out threads for me has been sitting and allowing the tears to come out so that I can heal and keep going.

As I drive these long hours, different scenarios come up for me again, some of which surprise me. There are certain triggers that remind me of moments of loss, transitions, seasons of life and people I miss deeply. As I name those feelings and the specific losses, I feel God's healing and as a result I feel more whole. I sense my perspective of the event shifting from despair to gratitude. Naming things is important.

As I was reminded in Arizona, God is big and I can trust God. This is a truth that I continually need to be reminded of. I can trust God with my feelings. I can bring my memories before God and receive healing and restoration. It's not always an easy or fast process, but I am thankful that each step is significant.

I am also thankful that God heals me in places beyond my awareness - through memories, feelings or events that I cannot always put into words. While there is value to naming things, I also recognize that God works much deeper within me as I am open to God and God's work in my soul. All of this ties into the mystery and wonder of who God is. As memories continue to surface and feelings keep rising up, I will continue trying to name them, knowing that God is present with me in those moments and desires to bring continued healing. God is good and continues to heal that which I am willing and able to name, and offers grace to the places that are still too painful to name.

9

Texas

You say Texas, I say tacos. Unlike in Idaho, my expectations in this area were actually correct.

There is great creativity in tacos and a plethora of ways they can be eaten. They also uniquely represent hospitality. I visited my friend Terra in Texas and enjoyed my time with her and her family immensely. It was my second time being in Austin and there was something special about returning to a familiar place. I had the privilege of being invited to share with their home church some of what I have learned throughout my life concerning loss and lament and then specifically about what I have been learning along the way on my trip.

It's funny to listen to yourself answer questions, because sometimes I'm a bit shocked at how profound and true my answers are. They resonate deeply and encourage me as I hear myself share them. It sounds funny but often we forget or don't fully notice the things that God has been doing within us or how we are being transformed and healed. I am often surprised and encouraged by my own courage in walking forward, and to see where it has led me. It is only in taking time to look back that we can see how far we have journeyed. This backward reflection becomes a source of hope.

I think this is why it's so important to share with others. It's one thing to process life on your own and be self-aware, but there is deep value in sharing it and encouraging one another. There is great value in hearing one another's stories and perspectives and using them as places to grow. Once in counselling, I was told that I was good at processing on my own in my journal, but that I needed to learn how to "journal out loud" with others, as a way of inviting others into my healing journey, and as a way of being vulnerable in the moment.

I met Terra when I first started seminary four years earlier. At the orientation, she was one of the first people I met when she came to sit at my table. I'm so thankful for a friendship that began so naturally, for a friendship that has continued to grow throughout our years of classes, meals and discussion together. I have learned a lot from her and how she has courageously walked through loss and continues to pursue God, her calling and meaningful community. My life is enriched by sharing life with her. Our time in Texas was spent with her house church, enjoying tacos, checking out some local spots and chatting in the coolness of a river on a hot day.

I need to continue sharing my story, and dedicate time to hear the stories of others, the good, the hard and the ugly. My hope is that there is value in it for others but also for myself, to remember and remind myself of what God has been doing. It is easy for me to get caught up in a moment and forget about God's faithfulness. God has always been present and faithful. I cling to this truth: as I have known it in the past, it is true for the present and will be true in the future. The truths that are clear in the light, on the sunny, beautiful days, are also true in the dark, but often we need extra reminders of those truths on the difficult days.

After Texas, there was a long stretch by myself and that makes me even more grateful for the richness of community and for people to share it with. So, I will continue to share my story and encourage others to share theirs. I will continue reflecting on what God has been doing and how I see myself being transformed and will continue to pursue God in all facets of this journey.

10

Oklahoma

"Oklahoma... where the wind comes sweepin' down the plain. O-K-L-A-H-O-M-A!"

"Noooooooo!" I yell at myself through my laughter, in response to me singing the same line from the musical, 'Oklahoma' for the hundredth time that morning. Are there no other songs written about Oklahoma that I can get stuck in my head? I chuckle to myself as I glance around at the dense forests around me. I guess the section of Oklahoma I chose to drive through is not the same place where the musical takes place in the plains. There are wind turbines though, so I guess there must be wind somewhere. Maybe it comes from the plains. The landscape is much different than I expected.

Expectations continue being a key theme on this trip and thoughts of them frequently swirl around my mind. I place a lot of expectations on myself and feel expectations from others. And if I'm honest, I project my expectations onto what God might expect of me. I have created space for this trip and want to honour it. I am so thankful for the opportunity to set this much time aside to go on a trip like this. Going on a 'grieving road trip' where writing is a big goal along with grieving is laden with expectations. How should I spend my time? What should I be thinking about? I'm reminded that I am where I am and that is okay.

I am where I am. This means that when my times of silence while driving through Oklahoma are obnoxiously interrupted with me singing the

Oklahoma song at the top of my lungs, it is part of the journey. This means being okay with stopping more to stretch my legs and rejuvenate myself when I'm feeling tired. This means paying attention to different emotions as they arise. And all those things are good and part of where I am.

My mind drifts to the book I've been reading by David Benner, 'The Gift of Being Yourself' where he posits that it is only when we accept ourselves exactly where and how we are that we can accept the fact that we are completely loved by God. There are certain parts of ourselves that we try to deny or push away because we want to change them. The desire for change is good but first we have to accept that it is the reality of our life and our current situations. If I merely live by my expectations, I will always fall short because I rarely live up to them.

Grief is laden with expectation. Based on our experience or what we have seen in the world around us, we form opinions on what it should be, how long it should take and how we should respond—nevertheless, it is a unique journey for each person. Where we are on the journey is where we are. There are certain places where we need to move forward, of course, but it's important to have grace with ourselves in the process.

I'm always annoyed when I watch a movie or TV show where someone is judged for not being "over" their grief. There seems to be an unspoken expectation of how long someone should be able to grieve and then life should resume as normal. News flash: life will never be normal again, because it has been horribly disrupted. It will look different moving forward, but the person who died will always be part of those who loved them and their loss will have a lifelong impact on each individual their life touched. This is okay. It also means that grief, however inconvenient and disruptive, is indeed a lifelong companion. There may be seasons where it is less intense and comes out in different ways, but when a life is altered forever, it has a lifelong impact. The only timeline that can be placed on grief is the length of one's life as we journey through the highs and lows, gifts and losses and weather each season and everything it brings.

My musical performance in my car (well, not a whole musical, but rather one song), has reminded me a lot of my brother Leon. He loved musicals and was an amazing performer. I feel tears rise within as I think about Leon and our shared love of musicals and how I would love to share a moment of singing with him again. I'm often surprised when grief arises over missing my brother, or even my dad, even though they died many years ago. Triggers for my grief happen unexpectedly and unpredictably. During these moments, such as attending a wedding, or seeing my nieces and nephews singing in their school concerts, the layers of grief leave me in a place of deep sadness. Sometimes this makes me feel weary about this journey I'm on because it seems like it never ends. How can I still be experiencing grief after all this time? There are people around me who would wish for me to move on, who would expect the passage of time to eliminate grief. Grief is complicated. It's not a straight and easy path. It is full of twists and turns, it loops back around to where you began, and its final destination is not always clear. It's not a linear journey through the five stages of grief, but is more closely related to chaotic scribbles swirling back and forth between all the stages. We form new normals and life is experienced as good again, but there is always the foundation of what we have lost and whom we carry with us in the legacies they left behind.

I'm continually letting go of my expectations and noticing where I am. It's a good place. It's a hard place. It's a grateful place. It's a constantly shifting place. It's an unpredictable place. Sometimes it's what I might have anticipated and other times I am completely surprised. Where I am is where I am and that's the best place for me to be. And at this moment, I'm in Oklahoma, so I will sing.

"Oklahoma… where the wind comes sweepin' down the plain. O-K-L-A-H-O-M-A!"

11

Arkansas

Have you ever had a moment when you thought you were smarter than your GPS? I like to consider the navigation on my GPS as a mere suggestion, deceiving myself into thinking that my navigation capabilities are far superior than the thing that was created solely for the purpose of giving me directions. Spoiler alert: I am not smarter than my GPS. Arkansas was kind enough to remind me of this fact.

Arkansas has always intrigued me because of its name. Kansas is pronounced with the s but Arkansas is pronounced with a 'w' sound at the end. Well, after a quick Google search, I learned that Kansas was the English spelling of a Native American tribe whereas Arkansas is the French spelling of a similar tribe. Regardless, every time I saw it written, I would say "Arkansauce" to myself and chuckle at how funny I was. I think this is a sign of me being by myself for too long.

I digress. Arkansas was lovely. I drove through the Ouachita Mountains on my way to Hot Springs (fun fact: this is where Bill Clinton grew up and when I first found that out, I tucked it into my memory in case it ever comes up in trivia).

My nightly road trip routine has been to pull out my map to see where I'm going the following day. In the morning, I plug my destination into my GPS and then highlight the route on my map as I drive. Although my GPS hasn't been updated in a while, it knows its stuff. It knows good routes to take and always guides me to my destination. The GPS has one job: to lead people to the correct destination.

Ironically, I experience a continual lack of trust in my GPS. I am travelling to new places. I don't know the roads. I don't know the best routes. I don't have a built-in knowledge of the best routes to take. I have a GPS so it can give me directions and guide me. So, it's obvious that I would know the routes and ways to go better than my GPS. I couldn't have pointed Arkansas out on a map to you before this trip and I still wouldn't be able to tell you how all the states are connected, and yet I am more trustworthy in directions than my GPS.

This being said, my GPS sometimes leads me on strange side roads because technically the distance is shorter. This happened a few times in Arkansas. I went on these back roads and 20 kilometres later they connected back to the highway I had been on. The speed limits were slower and the roads a bit bumpier, but to be honest, I was so thankful for these roads because the landscapes were beautiful and I enjoyed being forced to drive at a slower pace and take it all in. There were fields, trees, farms, abandoned houses, and rivers. It was lovely. So, even when it seems to be leading me astray, it is often the better route. Mind you, the other day when it asked me if I wanted to include unpaved roads on my trip, I kindly declined.

After walking around Hot Springs, I decided to drive around a bit more. I ended up on some back country roads and figured I would find my way back to town by following the signs leading me to Hot Springs Village. My GPS kept yelling at me to turn around (okay, she doesn't actually yell, but is very persistent in telling me to 'make a legal U-turn'), but I knew better. I knew this route would bring me back to where I wanted to be. Hot Springs Village, by the name, was obviously probably a small village right beside, or perhaps even nestled within Hot Springs. They were most likely the same place. I figured she (because spend enough time with your GPS and it becomes personified) would eventually come around and re-calculate according to my new (and better) route. Forty minutes later I finally decided to check out the map and see where I actually was. Turns out I had driven forty minutes out of town en route somewhere else and that Hot Springs Village is a different place than

Hot Springs. I had to drive back forty minutes the exact way I had come. Surprise! The GPS was right.

This is one of those "jolt of lightning" reminders that I'm not always right and I don't always have the best route or plan in mind. It's good to listen to others and to listen to God. I can trust the One who created me, knit me together in my mother's womb and knows every detail of my being. I'm in an interesting season of transition right now as I look ahead to the Fall. I am no longer a caregiver for my mom, I am moving out of an intense season of grieving and the options before me seem endless. I have been trying to plot my own way even though I continually feel led in specific directions. Sometimes those directions don't make sense to me, so I decide I should probably take a different turn because I know better (even though I have a very limited perspective of life). I need to trust the process. I need to trust the turns that don't seem to make sense but end up being the best possible way I could have gone. I need to slow down and be okay with bumpier roads. Besides, the bumpier roads are usually more interesting, beautiful and laden with adventure.

So, I will continue moving forward and trusting. Even when the road of grief feels long and weary, I won't try to take a shortcut, but will be faithful in walking the way that is before me. I will keep showing up, day after day. I will continue to remind myself that I don't know everything and I can trust God in the process of where my next steps lie. I will continue listening to others around me who have different perspectives and have perhaps been this way before. I will continue to keep my eyes and ears open to be amazed at what is on the road all around me. Whichever way I go, I trust that it is transformative, regardless if I can see the physical evidence of it. And I need to extend grace to myself in the moments when I forge my own path and ignore the clear one in front of me. I'm feeling reluctantly thankful for this journey and all its twists, turns and surprises.

12

Mississippi

One of my favourite places to visit while travelling are cemeteries. Strange perhaps, but a trip somewhere that includes walking around a cemetery brings me great joy.

So, when I visited Vicksburg in Mississippi, I was pretty excited to see that they have a number of different cemeteries full of rich history and stories of people who have been part of that history. They have a national cemetery that sprawls across their national park, honouring those who lost their lives in battle. I drove around visiting various cemeteries, walking around and taking in the depth, wonder and beauty that can be found in a cemetery.

This may seem strange to you. I can't fully articulate all the reasons why I love cemeteries so much. There is great mystery in it but as I continue to visit them, I understand their depth and value even more.

Cemeteries contain history. They represent people who lived and impacted the world around them in a plethora of ways. They are memorials to the stories of individuals and their families. They speak to the legacy that follows one's life.

When I'm in really old cemeteries, I am always struck by the depth of loss that some families went through. Lots of families are buried together and so, multiple family members and the dates of their deaths are listed on one grave plot. Too many children died too soon. Parents died, leaving children behind. Amidst all this loss, life has gone on. Perhaps some family members followed closely after others, but there was life amidst the loss.

Each name represents grief and loss. It represents an individual who was deeply loved and significant. Grief is a lonely road on many levels because one's grief process will depend on oneself but also on the type of relationship with the person who died. It is a unique journey for each person. At the same time though, in a cemetery, there is a sense of shared grief. Others have known loss. Others have walked through loss. People have continued to live meaningful lives in the wake of death and sorrow. There is a shared grief in humanity . As I take in the tombstones and the loss they represent, I realize I am not alone in my grief. To be alive is to experience grief. It is one of the most common human experiences. My grief is connected with theirs and theirs with mine. I can bring my grief and the memories of those I have lost and weep with those who have wept before me, knowing that I am not alone.

There is deep hope in these places too. Love and life triumph. Cemeteries represent life, love and the journeys each of us embarks on. They are a testament to the ways in which our paths cross and the influence we have on those around us. Loss binds us together and reveals that we are connected - otherwise we would not feel grief in the face of loss.

Each tombstone represents an individual created in God's image whose legacy and impact continue beyond the grave. As I walk around, there is a sense of awe and respect for those who have lived before me, for those who have lost before me. I am thankful that I am not alone on the journey of grief.

Facing death is part of being able to engage life more fully. Cemeteries hold no pretense. They are not hiding or glossing over death. The reality of death is there and must be confronted. Acknowledging death and the truth that it does not have the last word, leads us to life. It leads us to deep hope.

I leave you with a poem from one of my favourite poets, John Donne:

Death, be not proud

Death, be not proud, though some have called thee
Mighty and dreadful, for thou art not so;
For those whom thou think'st thou dost overthrow
Die not, poor Death, nor yet canst thou kill me.

From rest and sleep, which but thy pictures be,
Much pleasure; then from thee much more must flow,
And soonest our best men with thee do go,
Rest of their bones, and soul's delivery.
Thou art slave to fate, chance, kings, and desperate men,
And dost with poison, war, and sickness dwell,
And poppy or charms can make us sleep as well
And better than thy stroke; why swell'st thou then?
One short sleep past, we wake eternally
And death shall be no more; Death, thou shalt die.

13

Louisiana

As I get older, I realize the deep significance of place. Quite often, this significance emerges in familiar places we frequent regularly, or in sacred spaces that have been meaningful in our lives, or even while travelling.

There is something to be said about being in a place. Emotions are evoked as we return to places that are full of memories, whether good or bad. It seems our bodies are even aware of it, especially when we return to the places where we can breathe freely again.

Simply being in a place with some level of familiarity can bring up emotions, often unexpected ones. There is a mystery to be found in those spaces that is often beyond our comprehension and awareness. We are affected by different places without always being aware of it or able to control it.

Although my awareness of the significance of place continues to grow, I was still surprised to encounter deep feelings in Louisiana although I've never been there. My mom went quite a few years ago and she came back laden with stories and pictures to share. She recounted her experiences and how she was impacted by them. She related, through deep laughter, various funny events that had taken place. She described the delicious food she shared and enjoyed. She loved New Orleans and whenever someone mentioned it, she would pipe up with glowing reports of her time spent there. I had heard the stories so many times, I was able to start recounting them as though they were my own.

Needless to say, I had great anticipation for my time in New Orleans. Although I wasn't a fan of the crazy party scene, I appreciated walking around the different areas, taking the trolley, eating beignets by the river, enjoying Creole and Southern dishes, listening to live jazz, being enthralled by people watching and pausing numerous times to take everything in.

As I walked around, it felt special and significant knowing I was walking on some of the streets my mom walked on. I looked into stores and guessed at things she had probably wanted to buy (and some of which she did indeed buy). I heard a running commentary in my head of what she would have observed and how she would have responded. She would have expressed her desire to take the cooking class advertised at the kitchen shop - she would have wanted to try gumbo at different restaurants to find out which was indeed the best. She would have gushed about the deliciousness of the beignets and po'boys. I had a deep longing to share my moments and pictures with her. I wish I could have texted her to tell her I kept thinking about her, because so much here was reminding me of her. We could talk about the things we experienced that were in common and what was different, and maybe even how the area had changed in the last few years. Even though I couldn't send that text, there was an internal acknowledgement of the fact that just by partaking in all these things that she had enjoyed, I was sharing them with her.

One day I went on a swamp tour and got to see alligators and explore a bayou. Although I don't think my mom went on a swamp tour, I could imagine what her comments would be. Memories flooded back from our time in Kenya and Tanzania and her commentary about the animals we saw.

"Oh wow, look at that lion. He has scratches all over him. He must have been in a really big fight."

"Do you guys see the marks on those hippos? I think they've been in a really big fight."

"That cheetah has a scratch on his face, probably from a really big fight."

Apparently animals fight a lot. It seemed only natural to conclude the same for the alligators. I chuckled inwardly, as her voice ran through my head, commenting on the big fights that were probably had by the alligators, wild pigs, swamp canaries and giant spiders I saw. Any blemish on them was clearly due to a fight.

I imagined her commentary as we floated past the houses built on stilts right along the water. She would have speculated all the reasons why they were on stilts and would have wondered how often the water rises to the heights of the houses. On the way back, it poured rain and there was a big thunderstorm. I got soaked but it all felt like part of the experience of being there. I heard echoes of my mom's laughter in the rain, thinking about that time when we had broken out in peals of laughter when we got caught in a downpour while travelling together.

The next morning I visited Oak Alley Plantation. Everything was quiet when I arrived, as I was the first visitor. I walked out to the front oak tree walkway. Tree limbs on either side stretched out to one another, creating a perfect archway. The air was still and fresh with a new day. Suddenly I saw a family of foxes run out from under one of the trees. Six of them. They were running around and playing with one another. I stood in the stillness and quiet, watching them. Later they ran into their fox hole which was under one of the giant oak trees. Standing there watching them wrestling on the lawn was again one of those suspended moments filled with deep delight and God's presence, another place and moment to remember and cherish.

Walking through the plantation grounds and house and hearing all the stories also made me miss my mom. Her narration could be heard in my memories and imagination as I pictured what she might have said. She would have absolutely loved the beauty of the trees and the history of that place told by all the different perspectives of those who had passed through there.

I am adding all my new memories from Louisiana to the memories I hold that my mom passed on to me. The part of her legacy that lives on in me once again took everything in and treasured it.

I am so thankful for the significance of place: those I have been to a thousand times, and those I am discovering for the first time, yet following in the footsteps of those who have gone before me. These are memories I will hold dear.

14

Florida

For most of this trip, each time I wake up, I experience a moment of deep disorientation. I realize I'm either sleeping at a friend's house or in a hotel but I always pause as I collect myself, trying to remember where I am. Generally I list about five states in my head, wondering if that's where I am. Am I there now or was that yesterday? Am I there now or am I just anticipating heading there tomorrow?

Spending hours driving through each state is helpful in grounding me a bit more to where I am. In a world where transportation is much quicker and easier than it once was, we can be transported from place to place quite rapidly. The fact that I can travel to all the states in a condensed amount of time speaks to this phenomenon. As annoying as this disorientation feels, it's the perfect reflection of grief.

Transitioning from one place to another is a significant movement. It has an impact on our physical bodies, emotions, minds, and our spiritual beings (in short, it impacts us completely and fully). It is important to mark these transitions. It is easier for us, however, to pass through each phase and transition and simply look ahead to what is next. This will likely be accompanied by wondering why angst or other feelings seem to be building up because we haven't paid attention to the transition we have made.

Throughout my travels, I have found that taking photos, posting photos, journaling and blogging have been key in marking these transitions to each new place. I try to stop at each visitor centre to take a picture with their state sign. I talk to strangers wherever I stop and ask them about where they live, listen to pieces of their stories and often hear how they have experienced and walked through grief in their lives.

Driving through Florida was a really long driving day. I saw the Gulf of Mexico for the first time and drove along its coast. I enjoyed finding shapes in the cloud formations in the sky. I soaked in the beauty of the dark and brooding skies warning of coming rain. I loved the intermittent pounding rain as I drove. I was in awe at the beauty of the sunset through the mix of rain and clear skies. I was delighted by the different types of trees along the road. I pulled over whenever I saw something interesting and enjoyed the feeling of moving my leg muscles again.

I arrived at my destination on the coast really late. After a mishap at check-in (apparently they had cancelled my reservation without telling me), I dropped into bed and slept soundly. When I woke up the next morning I was in a blur as to where I was. To get to Florida I drove through Louisiana, Mississippi and Alabama and so it made sense that it took me a while to remember I was in Florida.

I went for a long walk on the beach. I hugged a couple palm trees. Walking was a good means for grounding myself in the place where I currently was, allowing my body to catch up with myself, and to continue processing all that has been in my heart and mind as I have gone along. It was helpful in giving myself space to be fully present where I was and to soak it all in.

Grace and space are vital as we transition from one place to another. Whether this be grief and loss, and processing everything that comes with it, or a regular transition of life from one season to another, it is important to mark these moments and to recognize that they will often have an impact on us far deeper than we initially perceive. We often rush through and forget to give ourselves time to catch up. One day I was in Louisiana and the next day I was in Florida. And the next day I was in Georgia.

15

Georgia

I wake up in a foggy state of heaviness. The day I have been dreading is here: Mother's Day. I want to hate today. In fact, it would be easy for me to hate this day. But I want to celebrate my mom today and I'm so excited to be in Savannah, Georgia. I tentatively get out of bed, open the blinds and it's a beautiful sunny day. The blue skies and sun feel like a taunt to the heaviness that this day brings, while simultaneously stirring hope within. Maybe this day won't be so hard after all.

I unlock my phone and open Instagram. My feed is filled with posts and pictures of children and their moms. My knee jerk reaction is to want to turn off my phone right away and spend the rest of the day filled with resentment and cynicism, feeling as though I have nothing to celebrate today. Maybe I could close the blinds and stay in my hotel room, hiding for the day. It would be easy to be filled with emptiness and anger in response to so many beautiful posts. It would be easy to be solely consumed in my own sadness.

These responses, however, would only bring harm to myself.

Yes, Mother's Day is a really hard day. It is a reminder of what I have lost. It is full of bittersweet memories of amazing time spent with my mom mixed with the longing to have her with me again. To add to my feelings of grief, it's also a reminder that despite longing for it, I don't have my own children to be a mother to. At times I feel alone in the middle, with no one to anchor me on either side of this day.

I miss my mom. Looking at pictures of her and I always brings back wonderful memories. Weekly movie night where we enjoyed Chinese food together. Driving around and hunting for grapefruit that was hanging over the walls of people's properties in Palm Springs. Playing games into the wee hours of the morning. Me slipping and falling and her laughing so hard and trying not to pee her pants. That time we thought we were whale watching in Hawaii but ended up on a historical boat tour instead. Riding giant stuffed motorized pandas in China. Hiking up Mount Sinai at 3AM in Egypt to watch a sunrise while being followed by men incessantly offering us camel rides. Snorkelling together in Galapagos Island when she suddenly had a moment of panic upon seeing the eels I was showing her, and shoved me into the coral reef to get momentum to swim away faster.

All of these memories and more are wonderful and yet they are filled with deep sadness. There is a gaping hole that pangs for her. I long to be enfolded in her deep, unconditional love. My body aches to be held in the grips of her giant hugs, that always lasted extra long. My ears strain to hear the depth of her full laughter. My heart wishes it could tell her again how much she meant to me, how deeply I loved and appreciated her. My passenger seat remains empty and oh how I wish she could be sitting there, joining me on my road trip adventures. This day is filled with deep sadness and longing.

But to focus solely on the sadness and longing would be a deep injustice, not only to the memory of my mom, but also to this day. I grieve deeply because I was loved, and loved deeply. The depth of my sadness reflects the depth of the relationship I shared with my mom. So today I want to choose to celebrate. I celebrate the 30 years I was blessed with the most wonderful mother. I remember the fun times and the hard times we shared that brought us closer together. I smile and laugh as I recount the memories. There is sadness, yes, but it is accompanied with a deep joy. There are tears, yes, but they are mixed with laughter.

Amidst the longing I feel on Mother's Day for my mom, I am also filled with deep appreciation and love for those who have influenced and invested in my life. For friends and mentors who have poured into me, loved me, believed in me, encouraged me and walked with me. I am thankful for spiritual mothers along the way. I'm thankful for those who have welcomed me into their families. I'm grateful for those who have expressed motherly love and concern. I'm thankful that a mother's heart can be expressed in so many different ways and can extend to so many people. My heart is full on many levels.

I am also deeply grateful for all the mothers I know who have taught me about life and God. I am thankful for how they have been images of God's love. I admire the daily sacrifices they make as mothers. I am grateful to journey with them through life and the different seasons of motherhood. I'm thankful for friends who are willing to share their little people with me, giving me opportunities to invest and play.

I also grieve alongside others who have lost their moms. I grieve alongside those who have lost their children. I grieve with those who have complicated relationships with their mothers, or never had the opportunity to know them. I grieve alongside those who long to be mothers.

Mother's Day is a day that brings up a myriad of emotions. Thankfully, sadness isn't the only one. And so I choose to smile, cry and laugh—to remember. I choose to grieve and celebrate.

With all these thoughts and feelings swirling around my mind and heart, I leave the blinds open, and I set out to explore Savannah. While I'm excited, I also am realizing I know nothing about Savannah, or where I should go. With a quick stop at the tourist information booth, I find a self-guided walking tour and decide to embark on it. The map has countless squares and parks, so I set out for one of them. Passing by other parks, I see benches and people on benches, just sitting and enjoying the day. There's the bench from Forrest Gump. There are kids running around the bench, playing. At each turn, I see families celebrating their mothers. Anger and debilitating sadness threaten to overtake me, but I remind myself, 'Today is a day to grieve while also celebrating. I miss my mom, but I'm not bereft of love and life isn't hopeless and defined by despair.' I suspect this will be the thing I tell myself throughout today.

I walk, I hear the birds chirping from the trees, I feel the breeze gliding through the streets. I walk. I enjoy the shade from countless trees as a brief reprieve from the humidity and the sweat dripping down my back. I walk.

There is a beautiful park with a fountain in the middle that is idyllic. I walk. There is a brick walkway by the river. I walk down to explore the lower part of town.

"Hello. Happy Mother's Day."

"Have a great Mother's Day, Ma'am."

As southern charm would have it, every single person I pass is wishing me a Happy Mother's Day. I smile and thank them. Normally this would have bothered me or been a continuous trigger point for tears throughout the day, but I'm allowing my smile to symbolize my mixture of thoughts. My smile conveys my sadness and how much I miss my mom. But it also symbolizes a celebration of cherishing so many amazing women who have filled the role of mother in so many loving ways. I think about these women along with my mom as I continue to wander the city.

I end the day at a small restaurant called 'Treylor Park'. A man named Trey started it and they serve spin-offs of trailer park food. When I walk in, I immediately love the eclectic decor and am overwhelmed by the smells of delicious food. My mom would have loved this place. I sit at a table and peruse the menu. In honour of my mom, I decide to branch out and try the peanut butter and jelly wings. Peanut sauce on wings dipped in peach jelly. Delicious. I lift my phone to take a picture. I am sad, because I used to love sending my mom pictures of food that I knew she would enjoy. I pause and take the picture anyway, imagining how much my mom would have enjoyed them.

After my delicious meal, I get up and start the walk back to my hotel. I'm glad I left my hotel room today. The day had its hard moments, but it wasn't as bad as I thought it would be. Maybe Mother's Day isn't the worst day after all.

16

South Carolina

I stopped at a few different places in South Carolina.

My first stop was Charleston. It was like Savannah in its abundance of fountains, parks and trees. The beach stretched for miles, with a boardwalk in the distance to walk over the water. As I walk down the streets of some of these older cities, it amazes me how much history is contained in these places. I am in awe of the feet that have walked these paths before me. It is a history filled with tragedy and celebration, death and life, discoveries and loss, justice and injustice, ambition and discouragement. So many events and emotions have their marks on these places. As I discover and explore, I am also adding my own story to this history.

For lunch in Charleston, I decided to eat local and ordered fried green tomatoes and grits. Grits are one of those foods that I have often heard about but have no idea what they are. Well, it turns out I'm not a huge fan (no offence if they are your favourite thing ever, they just weren't for me). However, now when someone mentions grits, I will be brought back to that open air restaurant where I enjoyed my fried green tomatoes, and watched people in the market. It is interesting how memories become imprinted on us. There are multiple aspects of my life where my memories are unclear, but perhaps it's because I didn't allow myself to sit in those moments, allowing them to become imprinted. I'm in too much of a rush to get to the next thing.

I loved the pineapple fountain in Charleston. Pineapples are a symbol of welcome in the south and judging by the plethora of pineapple decorations, I felt very welcome. At the plantation in Louisiana that I visited, they said it was a sign of welcome, and they would often cut it up for their guests, but when their guests had overstayed their welcome, they would find an uncut pineapple on their bed and this would be a (slightly passive-aggressive) way of saying please leave as soon as possible (and take the pineapple with you). I will now view pineapples differently but with a bit more meaning and more added memories.

When I'm in cities I like to go off the beaten track a bit. So in Charleston, I walked a bit farther out of town and ended up in some historic areas with really old houses. There were different people out and about on their porches and it was great to chat with them. After the day of walking around, I drove to Myrtle Beach where I enjoyed a long walk on the beach, dinner on the pier and then I sat on a tube in the lazy river run at my hotel. The Harley Davidson bike rally happened to also be in town, and I loved meeting and talking with a variety of people in the pool area and hot tub. It reinforced my opinion that hotel hot tubs are one of my favourite places to meet people. It is the most unexpected place to have random and good conversations and to be able to hear parts of people's lives and stories. Somehow I started talking with one couple about Christmas cards and we both shared how we have epic Christmas picture cards we send out, so we exchanged addresses to be able to send our Christmas photos to each other. I love random and unexpected interactions with strangers. They give me hope and a glimpse of the beauty of life and shared humanity and being able to celebrate humanity with others.

That evening I received a message from a friend from Ontario. I hadn't seen this couple in about five years and turns out they were in Myrtle Beach. So the next morning, we had a short visit on the beach. I often fail to notice the little things that are gifts from God, but how great to see how God connects our paths together.

I stopped in Greenville to visit my friend Becky for a couple days. Becky and I met at school in Portland and I'm so thankful for the gift of her friendship. We had fun walking around Greenville, going out for some tasty meals, and talking a lot. After having spent over a week by myself, it was great to have the contrast of being with someone and enjoying laughter, deep conversations, discussions and shared stories. Visiting different people on this trip has been a snapshot of all those who journey with me in different ways. I'm overflowing with gratitude at not being left on my own, but of having others to walk with and share life with. I could not do this journey alone and am so thankful for the panoply of amazing people along the way. We are not meant to live this life alone.

17

North Carolina

Does my life make an impact? Each funeral I attend becomes a mirror looking in on my life. At my mom's funeral, I remember being inspired by her hospitality and love for others. At my dad's, his generosity and charisma encouraged me. At my brother Leon's funeral, I was blown away by how many people were there, people whose lives had been touched by his life. His authenticity and ability to be with others motivated me. The impact of their lives is carried on through my life and is added to my own impact. What is my legacy and what will I be remembered for? I often wonder about the purpose of my life and if I'm going in the right direction. When I hear stories of other people's lives, it is inspiring but can also be discouraging if I fail to recognize that I'm a different person who has a different sphere of influence and impact based on the uniqueness of who I am and where I am. In North Carolina, I had this experience while walking through the Billy Graham Library in Charlotte.

The Billy Graham Library is the location of Billy Graham's childhood home and there is a big barn/museum used to share Billy Graham's story and how God used him throughout history and continues to use him today. The museum felt larger than life. The displays were very dynamic, well laid out and informative.

I had a lot of mixed feelings while walking through the museum. I laughed at the beginning of the museum when I was greeted by Bessie, the talking robot cow. The intricacies of each display struck me and wondered how much it must have cost to build. It is a bit baffling how much money is poured into certain things in the western evangelical world. Then again, they have a clear mission to share Christ with people who come and visit and have pursued excellence in creating a state of the art facility for this. It also brings up lots of feelings about evangelicalism, which throughout history has developed layers and layers of meaning. It was interesting processing and thinking about my own journey of faith as I walked through Billy Graham's journey and how he in turn shared it with the world. Whether I love everything about it or not though, Christ is being proclaimed and I can trust that the Holy Spirit will continue speaking to and using those who have heard the message about Christ through Billy Graham and his various ministries.

Regardless of one's thoughts or opinions, it is amazing to see what one man's faithfulness can become. Step by step he was faithful to what he felt God had laid before him and he continued stepping forward in complete trust and faith. When I see the breadth and depth his ministry has had, it is astounding and encouraging. There were moments where I had to fight the temptation of comparing my life with Billy Graham's. Sometimes I wonder what my life has amounted to, where it is headed and whether it will affect others in the future. Have I squandered it? Am I living to my full potential? On this trip it has been a question that has come up frequently, especially as I have been writing. What is this all for? Is this important and significant? Is this how I should be spending my time? I tend to get caught up in trying to track my impact to make my life meaningful. I've walked through difficult things. I don't want it to be wasted.

My life will likely never be like Billy Graham's, and that's okay. In fact, it's probably a very good thing since I am not Billy Graham. The things I am being invited into are completely different and unique to who God made me to be. God is calling me to be faithful in the things that have been placed before me. This often feels intangible, making the shift in perspective difficult. I strive for measurable results and evidence of meaning. I don't generally see it and that's probably a good thing. I'm reminded of the fact that even if just one person is impacted by my life, then that is enough. In some situations maybe it will be me that's changed and that is enough. My life is enough.

The evidence of Billy Graham's impact on life is far clearer than for most of us. This doesn't make our lives any less significant or meaningful. I can celebrate what God has done through Billy Graham while celebrating that this is the same God who is continually transforming and using me. My prayer is that I would be used and that my life would glorify God in the unique way that only my life can. I often wonder if I'm doing the right things or making the right life decisions. Yet, where I am is where I am. It is easy for me to get caught up in trying to figure it all out rather than actually being where God has placed me, being faithful to what is directly before me. I don't need to manufacture meaning out of my life. I am called to be faithful and show up and be me in every moment and circumstance. God is faithful. God has always been faithful. I can trust that God will continue to be faithful.

18

Alabama

You can probably guess what song was stuck in my head for three days straight.

One of the things I love about road trips is that each moment of the journey is a destination in itself. There is always something to see and discover. En route to Alabama, I stopped at the Martin Luther King Jr. National Monument and then drove through some beautiful mountains crossing from Georgia into Alabama. The landscape is always inspiring, with moments of beauty along the way. A few scenic turn-offs had me laughing at the fact that they were just really tall trees and you couldn't see a thing. Nonetheless, I still felt compelled to pull over at every single one, just in case.

In Alabama, I visited my friend Brett and his family. As soon as I arrived, we went to a really cool event called 'Stories under the Stars.' The location was perfect. It's on the top of a hill, at the location of an old mansion and the views stretch for miles. There's a large grass area to sit and take in the view while listening to the stories. Super cool idea, except most of the stories sucked. We sat there feeling awkward for the person telling the story, because they weren't good storytellers and they were nervous. Their stories became pointless ramblings that detracted from their actual story.

The few good stories, however, made me reflect on the art of telling a good story. The unfortunate part is that those who weren't the best storytellers had decent stories to share, but the way they shared the story ruined it. Every time I meet someone new (or someone I know), there is an opportunity for sharing part of my story. I love the art of storytelling and desire not only to live a good story but to be able to share it in ways that are intentional and meaningful. Less is sometimes more.

The next couple days included multiple activities: fishing, exploring Cathedral Caves, eating BBQ by the river, eating catfish by the river, eating sandwiches by the river (definitely an important theme of enjoying good food in good company in beautiful places). I also got to shoot a gun for the first time as a way of rounding out my American experience.

There's deep value in sharing experiences with others. Much of this trip has been on my own and I have appreciated that for many reasons, but the contrast of time alone and time with friends reminds me of the richness of sharing life together. There is something special in being able to make memories and have shared experiences with other people. I also feel the weight of grief as I create new travel memories. Growing up we travelled a lot as a family, and then my mom and I travelled extensively and I have a lifetime of memories from those trips. I am the sole holder of those memories now, and it hurts to not be able to share them with her. These have been some of the unexpected, ongoing aspects of grief that arise when I least expect them to. In those moments, the significance of sharing stories is even more profound, knowing that I don't have to silently hold these memories by myself. In telling the story, it lives on in the hearts and minds of those who have heard it.

19

Tennessee

"Someone I loved once gave me a box full of darkness. It took me years to understand that this, too, was a gift." - Mary Oliver

Darkness.

It's a word we often associate with the negative. The word itself conveys something we want to avoid. Darkness makes us yearn for light. We try to escape darkness. We turn on lights in our homes at night, we turn on lights in our vehicles when we drive, we bask in sunlight. After long, dreary and dark days of winter, we long for spring and dream of long summer days filled with sunshine and light.

My time in Nashville was great. I enjoyed walking around the city, exploring and discovering different areas, but it felt obscured by an internal darkness. This darkness had nothing to do with Nashville, but it just happened to be the moment where I felt the darkness deeply. I felt a heaviness and a deep sadness and it was difficult to see anything beyond it. I had to work extra hard to notice the good things in the day and to take in what I was seeing. I was completely exhausted by the end of the day.

The hard reality is that darkness is destructive. Plants die and shrivel without sunlight. Hiking paths become treacherous for the hiker. Beautiful landscapes are rendered to blackness. Life struggles to thrive.

I only endured darkness in Nashville for one day. But in the past couple years, I could not escape darkness. My life was steeped in darkness. I often felt stuck in it. All was silent. I didn't know where I was or where I was going. I couldn't see anything around me.

I have labelled this season of life as winter. The irony is that, in nature, this is my favourite season. When I lived in Quebec, the winters were very long, and my longing for spring was very great. And yet when I stopped to look at winter, at all its wonders, I saw much beauty and richness. But a spiritual winter? It's hard for me to see its beauty, its richness.

Over the last few months I have been transitioning into spring. And as I reflect back on the darkness and barrenness of my long winter, I am thankful now that I did not rush through it or try to avoid it. As much as I didn't want it to be true, the darkness of winter has been necessary. Painful and messy, yes. Heart-wrenching and tearful, yes. Isolating and lonely, yes.

But healing, too. Staying in the darkness allowed me to cling to God and discover a hope I could only find in God. Walking through the darkness gave me deeper trust. Sitting in the darkness allowed me to feel God's comfort and presence.

All along, in the darkness, a crucial transformation was happening.

Of course, in the midst of it, I didn't see or understand this. I clung to a hope for it, but I couldn't see past the pain. But now looking back, I see it, a little at least, the gift that the darkness was.

I often tried to escape to find the light. When I was 18, I was in a season of darkness. My brother had died two years earlier, followed by my dad a year and a half later, followed by both my grandparents on my dad's side. I was faced with grief, but I did not give myself permission to grieve, nor did I know how to process all the emotions that were rising up within me. I moved to Quebec in a desperate attempt to escape the darkness that threatened to consume me. I didn't know how to navigate the darkness. Yet it was artificial light I sought, refusing to work out what needed working out. I didn't take time to listen to my own sadness. I didn't take time to notice what the darkness had to teach me. I short-cut the process and robbed myself. Ironically, by running from the darkness, I made the road harder and longer for myself.

But finally, I took the time. I faced the darkness. I walked in it. I sat in it. Eventually, I walked through it.

Others faithfully walked and sat with me. Prayed with me. Prayed for me. Hoped with me. Longed for light with me. Now, I am thankful that I created and found spaces to sit in the darkness rather than avoid it or run away from it.

You see, the amazing thing is, things grow in the dark. Seeds germinate in darkness. A baby grows in a dark womb. A photo develops in a dark room. Sleep and rest happen behind the darkness of shut eyes. Life emerges in these unexpected places.

And just so, things within me started to grow. Healing began to take place. Transformation in me started, and continues. I don't say this to romanticize the darkness, but rather to urge you to cling to hope. Life emerges in places that feel lifeless.

Not all darkness is the same, I know. I'm simply sharing my own experience. When I say darkness, I don't mean evil. I mean what I've experienced: an isolating feeling of despair and general lost-ness. Maybe you can relate.

My word for 2016 was 'hope.' I undertook a 366-day photo project of pictures of light along with quotes about hope. This brought me, and still does, continual reminders that, although the darkness has a purpose, it does not have the last word. I am thankful, though, for how that darkness led me into this new season filled with life. I'm thankful for the perspective I have gained and will continue to gain. I'm thankful for healing (but I could only heal the things I allowed myself to express and recognize needed healing). I'm thankful, looking back, to see the many traces of light and hope that were present with me throughout the darkness, even though I did not recognize them at the time.

I hesitate to share these thoughts on darkness, because I recognize it might be misunderstood or misconstrued. But I share it because I want to testify to the transformation in my life. And I share it because I welcome continued conversation about these topics. I share it because sometimes we don't allow, even in our churches, space to sit in these hard places. We want to rejoice and be happy. We want to bask in the reality of Easter Sunday. We forget the darkness of Holy Saturday. We forget that sometimes we don't feel like we have any answers. We forget that life can be messy and painful. We forget to hold the tension of darkness and light together.

Here is a quote that I reflected on that evening in my hotel room in Nashville:

"When we so fear the dark that we demand light around the clock, there can be only one result: artificial light that is glaring and graceless and, beyond its borders, a darkness that grows even more terrifying as we try to hold it off. Split off from each other, neither darkness nor light is fit for human habitation. But if we allow the paradoxes of darkness and light to be, the two will conspire to bring wholeness and health to every living thing." - Parker Palmer

May your moments of darkness be places of growth. May they be wellsprings of life. May they lead you to deeper healing, more profound joy, and greater intimacy with God.

20

Kentucky

Things I associate with Kentucky: bourbon, fried chicken, baseball and the Kentucky derby. In general I prefer exploring beautiful places in nature, but every so often I enjoy exploring a city. In Kentucky, I visited Louisville.

I walked around a lot, visited both sides of the river (I snuck over to Indiana, although I'm not counting it yet) and enjoyed views of the bridges. I went to the baseball bat museum and factory and went bourbon tasting. I took pictures of some of the horse statues around town and ate some fried chicken. I did my part in reinforcing the four things that were already in my mind about Kentucky.

Each night I usually look up where I'm going to the next day and do some research on what I would like to do. Usually cities have a lot of different options and while looking stuff up about Louisville, I had become overwhelmed and frantic, wondering how in the world I would cram everything in. Out of nowhere, suddenly I became interested in multiple things that have never interested me. Their luring calls were tempting me because they seemed like good experiences, but maybe doing one thing I really enjoy is more worthwhile than ten things that I feel apathetic about. Or maybe picking one thing I want to learn more about is worth more than being saturated with way too much information that I won't remember anyway.

Giving myself more space to breathe and not cramming everything in has been a crucial theme over the last couple years. My mantra has become "Just because I can do something doesn't mean I should." My visits to different places keep reinforcing this as I realize that it's better to be fully present in a couple things that might connect with me more deeply than trying to accumulate endless experiences and information. Through grief, one of the biggest things I have learned is to extend grace to myself. Grace was my word for 2017 because I still needed constant reminders of this and needed to keep reflecting on grace, learning to abide in the grace that God continually extends to me.

When I initially became a caregiver for my mom, I realized things in my life needed to change, specifically how I spent my time. I was still in a pattern of saying yes to everything and did not want to miss out on any opportunity. Yet the emotional and physical energy that was required of me in taking care of my mom left me exhausted and spent. I made a list of the things that were really important to me and the things I didn't care much about. It became transformative to cut out the things that were not life giving and that I did solely out of compulsion and obligation. My time became more meaningful and rejuvenating, even in the things I did with my mom.

My day exploring Louisville was a great day. There's so much more I could have done and seen, but it was perfect because I was present and I enjoyed it and can see some other things the next time I go. I can be content with what is before me rather than trying to grasp frantically for more.

21

West Virginia

I know two things about West Virginia: it's a state and it is west of Virginia (I didn't look it up, but I'm assuming it's true). This information is helpful in locating the state but otherwise it's quite useless (especially if you also don't know where Virginia is).

Driving into West Virginia, I realize I have no expectations, because I know nothing about it. I am surrounded by lush and beautiful scenery. Everywhere I look, there seems to be a waterfall, or a grove of flourishing trees. I'm feeling pleasantly surprised, realizing that my lack of knowledge of this state had left me with minimal expectations. I find myself smiling continually in delight at my surroundings. I spot a cool-looking bridge ahead and pull over to take a closer look. As I step out of my vehicle, I inhale deeply, smelling the richness and beauty of the forest around me. I spot a path that I follow, leading me to a better view of the river. I continue my drive, enjoying the beautiful old brick churches and the simple beauty of winding roads alongside the river.

It's so rainy. This means more fog. Having already experienced fog in California, I'm over it. Yes, it's symbolic, but do I really need continual reminders of it? I think back to the significance of it and I'm reminded of the beauty in the obscurity during moments where I lack understanding and clear vision. Although I'm surrounded by beauty and good things today, I don't feel this. Fog feels like grief that has blanketed every fibre of my being, casting a dampness over everything that is good and beautiful, choking it out.

There are these moments where grief feels so all-encompassing and I can't see any distance in front of me. It feels like there will never be a way out and I will be trapped here forever. I know this is just a day and that it won't always feel like this, but it's hard to cling to that perspective when the weight of grief is crushing me.

And yet, fog beckons me to step forward, coaxing me to take another step. The next step is a step filled with a desperate need for hope and a promise of a different feeling in the future. Yes, fog feels a lot like grief, but for me, it also symbolizes the all-encompassing presence of God. This presence, though not physically tangible, is enveloping and all-consuming. I feel like my life is frequently lived in the fog, but I'm learning to see where the beauty lies. Some days this is much harder than others. It's not what I expected and yet the fact that it is shrouded in mystery adds depth to its beauty and intrigue. I guess it's not so bad to have another reminder of the fog, especially on a day when I feel the weight of grief. I'm present with it but continue moving forward.

We often go into situations overloaded with knowledge. We have seen photos and heard other people's experiences, thereby shifting our expectations and experiences because we hold them up to our preconceived notions of what something will be. Grief is universal and consequently we have a lot of preconceived ideas about it and create expectations for ourselves through grief. Yet each loss is unique to each individual experiencing the grief of that loss. Grief is unpredictable and is not tied down by our expectations. It would be easy to get frustrated with myself for feeling the deep, all-encompassing weight of grief during my drive through such a beautiful area. *I should be enjoying this more. I should not still feel grief this strongly. I should be able to have a better perspective on this.* But some days grief just plain sucks and you can't see past it. I give myself extra grace those days. I pause to notice things. I allow myself to feel deeply because I know it won't be forever. I also don't make big decisions those days. I don't always trust all my thoughts about myself or life, because grief has a way of skewing those as well. Grief rears its head at the most inopportune moments and tends to be quite disruptive. Let it be. It will show up, but it won't stay forever.

22

Virginia

Virginia: the state that is east of West Virginia. Okay, so it turns out there are a lot of states I know virtually nothing about. I know some people who live in those states, but otherwise they are just names I have heard from history, without remembering the details. I have heard about the Blue Mountains, but I had no idea they were in Virginia. I made a little detour to drive through the Blue Mountain Parkway and it was well worth the detour.

For part of the drive, it was pouring rain and once again there was fog at every turn, adding to the mystique and beauty of the place. I stopped at all the viewpoints. Some of them led to walks through the forest, leading me to lovely waterfalls and abandoned, overgrown train tracks. At the overlooks, there were signs talking about the mountains in the distance and other landmarks that I couldn't see. I imagined that the beauty I was seeing was also hiding a lot of the beauty behind the fog. Sometimes we just have to trust that there is indeed deep worth and beauty beyond what we can perceive and understand. I can't remind myself of this enough. The rain also made the forest quite lush and beautiful for the entire drive into Williamsburg.

I was going to Williamsburg to visit a friend and when I looked it up, I realized that in America's history, Williamsburg is a big deal, along with Jamestown. I'm hesitant to admit my ignorance of this part of history, but was pleasantly surprised at the chance to go exploring and wandering along the historic streets of Colonial Williamsburg and to go to the original site of

Jamestown. Needless to say, I learned more history and enjoyed being taken into a different "world" as I walked down historic streets and read about different people who had left their old lives behind and started new ones elsewhere.

I was in Williamsburg on Ascension Day and attended an Ascension Day service. I chose to sit in George Washington's pew. I know I've mentioned it before, but it's always so amazing to actually be in the same physical places where significant history has taken place, where people have lived and worshipped before me. I loved worshipping in a church that is different from my own and was deeply blessed by the service (even if there were a few times where I may have remained standing while everyone else sat down… the perks of being in the front row and not being able to see the people behind you. Thanks, George Washington).

In Jamestown, there was a large thunderstorm approaching and although my friend Tara and I were warned it was coming, we figured we could beat it. For the most part we avoided the rain as we hid in a museum to stop from getting wet. As a bonus, the museum had a bunch of skeletons that had been dug up on the site. We got to read the stories of some of the people who came to Jamestown and also to read some of the history of Pocahontas (not the Disney version). There is so much we can ascertain about those who have come before us and what their lives were like.

I felt connected to the people whose lives I was reading about, who inhabited these spaces as I encountered new places and history that I didn't even realize I would get to learn about. These are places that hold people's stories. What stories do I hold for others to carry on their legacies? Who holds my stories? How do I keep telling the stories of those who have gone before me?

One of the main ways I have determined to hold and share the stories of family members who have died is to use their birthdays and the anniversaries of the days they died in order to honour and remember them. Of course, my remembering isn't limited to these days, but I make it a point to do something on that day that they would have enjoyed. In memory of my dad, I will go golfing, cook Maui Ribs, or go to a restaurant we enjoyed together. In memory of my mom, I get some of her favourite food, or I get a peanut buster parfait from DQ (with caramel sauce added in). In memory of Leon, I go see musicals or something involving music, or I play a board game with friends. In memory of my grandparents, I go for a long walk, reflecting on special moments we shared together, or I make one of my grandmother's recipes. I invite others to join me who knew them too. I post photos and stories online, inviting others who knew them to share their own stories. These simple things become profound places of remembering and celebrating who each person was. I especially love reading a story that is new to me. These gestures seem small at times, and yet, I recognize the enormity of their importance and carrying on someone's legacy, celebrating a person's life, and inviting others to do so with us.

23

Maryland

Ten years ago, while travelling, my mom and I met a woman named Sammy. We enjoyed getting to know one another over dinner and over the years we have sporadically kept in touch. It turns out she lives in Maryland and I was able to visit her and meet some of her family.

Much of my trip has been filled with spectacular sights, beautiful nature, big cities, but one of the standout aspects is the people that I have been able to visit and reconnect with along the way. Life would be bleak if it were void of people. We were not created for isolation. We were created to relate to one another and build relationships with those around us. There is a rich tapestry of people who have been woven into my life, whether for a short time, frequently or periodically through the years. Different seasons of life shift relationships and each one has been meaningful, no matter the length of time. Visiting people who also knew my mom is bittersweet. I long for her presence with me there or I at least want to call her to tell her all about my visit. There is something special about being with someone who also holds stories and memories of someone who has died.

It's a curious thing to travel by yourself for long periods of time. I really enjoy time spent by myself but I also enjoy people. After leaving Maryland, I had ten straight days by myself. One of the layers of grief I have had to walk through is my feelings of being alone. Having no parents, no grandparents, no spouse and no children, sometimes it feels like I am adrift without anything anchoring or rooting me. I have a lot of amazing friends that share and celebrate life with me, but sometimes my moments feel scattered among my friends with no one who holds all of them. My mom was the person who heard and knew most of my moments, who tracked with me through life, checking in with me daily. I would share details of the day and pictures with her. It is hard to face the loss of a relationship that was so deeply woven into my life.

Sometimes this alone-ness feels like an endless pit inside of me that is impossible to fill. It distorts my thinking and overwhelms me with loneliness. Nobody understands me. No one is regularly in my life. I could slip through the cracks and nobody would notice. This, however, is not true.

Yes, I have deep feelings on this level of being alone. But when I stop to reflect, I am far from alone. Amazing friends and a rich community surround me. Even when they are physically absent from me, they support me, love me and cheer me on from a distance. Who knows what rich friendships the future holds. During my travels, friends have been sending random messages to say hello and to see how I'm doing. I'm thankful for those who have followed me and encouraged me along the way and cared about where I was and if I made it to the next location safely. My mom used to be this for me, but it doesn't mean it has to stop. It just means it will look different. Maybe being seen in different snippets of life by multiple people who love me isn't such a bad thing. It's just different. I will miss the gift of these friendships if I focus solely on what I don't have.

Social media often shows me pictures of other people's families and relationships. They look different from mine – they stir a longing within me to have what they have – but when I step back, I realize those relationships don't make mine less meaningful. Yes, they look different, but that's okay. I have people who love me, support me, affirm me, and cheer me on. I have people who have wept with me, laughed with me, walked with me through the darkest valleys and been willing to sit in the silence and loss with me.

So although my "official" family tree may have shifted, I am aware that there have been amazing people grafted, woven and embedded in the fabric of who I am and who I am becoming. I am not alone. It is so easy to overlook this. And yet even this trip has served as a reminder of it. I have someone I can visit in Maryland. I have people who have been significant parts of my life and I want to continue remembering and celebrating those people. I am far from being alone even when there's no one around.

<h1 style="text-align:center">24</h1>

Delaware and New Jersey

There are some states that I spent more time in than others. There are also some states where I took way more pictures. Some days I don't feel like taking pictures. Some days I'm "over" being on this trip and don't care about anything. I feel numb and disengaged and am just aiming to get through the day. Grief often feels like this. The days I spent in Delaware and New Jersey also felt a lot like this, mirroring my grief to me in many ways.

Making a plan to travel through all 50 states is no small task. It took hours of planning, mapping, re-planning, re-mapping, looking up interesting stops, coordinating dates with people I wanted to visit and figuring out how long each day would take and what was feasible driving time. Some days that are only three hours of driving turn into eight hours, because I like to pull over and follow signs on the road leading me to interesting places (or on the rare occasions totally uninteresting places that do not live up to their names). Two things I forgot to factor into my road trip planning were time changes and toll charges. Entering Delaware began my deluge of having to pay tolls in different areas.

In my planning and during my travels, one of the questions that has come up is what it means to be in a place. For me specifically the question is what does it mean to have been in a state. I have driven a few hours in every state I have passed through, enjoying the scenery along the way. I have usually had some sort of rest stop. I have eaten a meal in every state. I have taken a picture in every state. I've chatted with people in every state. Is it necessary to do something spectacular or see the main attraction to have been in a state or is it just enough to have physically been there and created your own experience?

If someone came to visit me in BC (British Columbia) and I picked them up at the airport and brought them to my house and they never set foot out of my house or did any activities, would they still have been in BC? My answer would be yes, but it would have been a different experience compared to someone who went back-country hiking in BC for 10 days.

Traditionally, my nature has been to tackle everything when I go somewhere. When I was 13, our first international family trip took us to Ireland for a few weeks. My mom researched everything there was to see and do in Ireland and we did it all. She rented a giant van (which is a horrible idea in a country with narrow, windy roads) and wanted to make sure we didn't miss anything in case we never had the chance to go back. I suspect this was where this way of thinking was born. And yet as I grow older, the truth keeps repeating itself: less is more. Just because there is a great experience to be had does not necessitate that I say yes to that opportunity. Sometimes moderation and saying no is a good thing and makes the other experiences even better.

Grief is similar in some ways. We have all experienced different types of grief depending on what we have lost. Life is full of loss. Our grief is influenced by things such as our personalities, previous losses and our expectations. We can learn from and grow from another's experience of a similar thing. A loss is a loss, no matter what it is. Grief cannot be measured and isn't just worthy of the big things in life. Day to day losses are important to grieve as well, so that we can continue moving forward and receive what is coming next.

Delaware and New Jersey are two states I would like to return to, because I feel like I missed out on some aspects of exploring and experiencing everything they have to offer. In many ways, we face them when we encounter people whose grief is at the forefront. In our interactions with those in the throes of grief, we can't take anything personally, because they are in a completely different space. I was not in a space to fully appreciate the beauty that Delaware and New Jersey had to offer. The gift I experienced here was being able to be present to my grief, and hopefully on my next visit, I can appreciate some of the aspects that I missed.

I have not seen everything each state has to offer, but I am being present wherever I am and taking in the experience that my itinerary in each state offers me. I'm glad for the rhythm of busier days and more relaxed days, and if I return to any of these places, I know there will be other things to see and do and that will be a new experience. My experiences in each state and being present where I am is good and worthwhile.

25

New York

Part I

Out of the two trips my mom and I planned to New York, both were disastrous yet had redeeming qualities. The first trip, I was getting over a lung infection and she had been recovering from bronchitis and a bad cough (I realize in retrospect this was likely her lung cancer already rearing its head). We were a hacking pair that could only take a few steps before being completely winded. It was her first time in New York, but because we had respiratory issues, we couldn't walk around much and needed more rest. We saw some musicals, went to a few famous chef restaurants that my mom really wanted to try out and then the rest of the time we hunkered down in our hotel room watching movies on the hotel TV. Although it was not the grand New York trip we had envisioned, a lot of fun was had that weekend and I have some great memories from our time together.

We didn't make it to New York on our second trip. My mom was flying to Montreal to meet me (I was living in Quebec at the time) and then we were going to fly to New York City together. We had just found out that there was the possibility she might have cancer so we weren't sure if she should risk travelling but being the adventurous spirit that she was, she wouldn't take no for an answer and insisted that we still go. On the way to Montreal, she almost died on the plane from a blood clot in her lung. So, she went straight to emergency from the plane, stayed there three days and was banned from flying for a week. While she was in the hospital I would bring her tasty Montreal food and we would play Yahtzee together on her hospital bed. Then she spent a few days with me at my place and I flew back to BC with her. This was not the New York trip we had planned and it included scary and sad moments as we anticipated what the future might look like once we got her full diagnosis. But through it all I still have fond memories of laughter and making the best of a situation that wasn't the most positive.

So, when I went to New York, my mom wasn't far from my mind. As I walked around Central Park, I was brought to tears thinking about the fact that she never got to see the park. I ate at some of the same restaurants and I saw some fantastic musicals that transported me into other worlds, left me crying and laughing and feeling inspired and hopeful about life.

I love musicals. My love for musicals is perhaps a bit over the top and obsessive but I see them every chance I get. When I was younger, whatever musical was in town, my mom would buy eight tickets (because that's how many seats her vehicle had), she would fill up her vehicle and we would all head to Vancouver to be dazzled and wowed by the different shows (and the odd time disappointed but with funny stories of a not-so-great show that we tediously endured together). She didn't always know the storylines, which meant I saw a lot of musicals at a young age that were not always age-appropriate (Miss Saigon, Sunset Boulevard, The Full Monty), but most of the inappropriate parts went over my head as I was drawn in by the music and dancing. She introduced me to musicals at a young age and fostered my love for them.

Although my whole family enjoyed musicals, I especially shared a love for them with my oldest brother, Leon. He was an amazingly gifted musician and he performed in some high school musicals. It is impossible to watch Fiddler on the Roof and to not picture Leon's shining moment as a bottle dancer. He was 6'4" and glided across the floor with grace and ease. It was such a joy to watch him perform and come alive doing something he loved and excelled at. One of my days in New York was the anniversary of the day Leon died. It seemed fitting to remember him by going to see musicals I know he also would have loved. I saw Waitress, Come From Away, Dear Evan Hansen, and Anastasia. Leon would have loved the music, storylines and variety of each show. My heart yearns to have been able to share these shows with him. I am continually surprised at the sadness that surfaces in these moments of missing him.

Each musical I saw was spectacular in its own way and spoke deeply to me and to different aspects of grief in unexpected ways. I love how stories can do this, especially stories that come at you in the form of singing, dancing and acting. Remembering my mom and Leon while there made it even more special, being able to honour them and their impact on my life.

Part II

About two weeks after my initial visit to New York in New York City (Part 1 of this chapter), I spent some time in upstate New York, in the Finger Lakes area. A casual driving day ended up being a formidable waterfall tour. I drove by roadside waterfalls, followed by a visit to Glen Watkins State Park, which is a river running through a gorge with waterfalls, some of which you can even walk behind. They had stone steps and bridges throughout the park so you could walk along the entire length of the gorge. I ended up getting soaked as I walked behind a couple of the falls but it was a refreshing reprieve from the humidity and worth it to be so close to something so majestic. The entire day felt filled with wonder and the continual gift of being able to enjoy one of my favourite things.

What I loved about the park was being struck with awe at each new point. I would lower my expectations but as soon as I turned a corner, I saw something different and wonderful in its own way. This is such a good picture to keep moving forward, and although the stairs with 100 steps in front of you seem daunting, it is worth it in the end. The stairs will end, the ground will be level. It won't always be so hard.

26

Connecticut

One of the things I love about this road trip is that when I see a sign for something interesting or random, I have the freedom to pull over and explore. Sometimes this leads me to a dead end. Other times I am pleasantly surprised. I have taken countless detours for beaches, trails, and waterfalls. And then there are random destinations, like the Pez Candy Visitor Centre in Connecticut. I might have been the only adult without children there, but for me, a road trip is not complete without a stop somewhere completely random and unexpected.

This trip has been filled with many grand sites. From stunning waterfalls to awe-inspiring canyons, to oceans, mountains and forests. Amidst the grandeur of it all, it can be easy to miss the small joys as well. If you had the choice between the Grand Canyon and the Pez Visitor Centre, I'm guessing you might choose the Grand Canyon (unless you're a die hard Pez collector of course). Yet the combination of both of these places have distinct memories in my trip and they play important parts. I'm quick to cast aside the "small" or ordinary things, missing their significance altogether. And yet each of these moments is woven into my tapestry of memories. Each plays a part in my journey and also in forming who I am. We often look to the big things or big decisions in life and yet it's often the incremental decisions or moments that make the biggest difference over time.

My childhood is filled with epic memories. My family went on many adventures and sometimes it felt larger than life. I remember the frantic feeling of running to the bathroom while gassing up on drives to California, because my dad didn't want to lose any time on the road. I feel the bumps we flew over while sand duning on the Oregon Coast. I feel the spray of the ocean on my face on a boat trip, waiting for the moment when my dad's newest pair of sunglasses would fly unexpectedly into the ocean. I remember days spent playing in the ocean in Hawaii. I remember feeling my mom's stress as she tried to navigate the narrow roads in Ireland in the monstrous van we had rented. I laugh thinking of my mom's commentary on our childhood home videos.

There are so many moments, big and small, that have been treasured as memories. Most often, though, it's the little things I remember about the people who have died. I remember playing in the woods with my brother growing up, listening to the stories his imagination would weave (he told me the Care Bears lived in the forest and I kept hoping they would come out to meet us and play with us). I remember the nervous excitement as I watched Leon throw a match on the paths of gasoline my brothers had poured around the driveway to see how it would burn, and wondering how angry my mom would be when she got home. I feel the pain of the bee stings after my brothers coerced me to retrieve my mom's cooking pots that they had put over a beehive. I remember regularly going out for meals with my dad and begrudgingly listening to his favourite songs (which would eventually become my favourites, too). I remember hanging out in the kitchen with my mom while she cooked. I yawn at the thought of all the late nights my mom, Leon, and I would spend playing games around the kitchen table. I'm tired thinking of all the times I would come home past 10 PM to my mom vacuuming the house. I remember our weekly Sunday bike rides where my dad would push me up the giant hills when I couldn't pedal up them myself (as an adult I realize how hard this must have been, especially since he was 6'5"). I remember dinners that my Oma would cook for us, putting so much love and care into each serving. I remember my Opa's one liners and sipping yerba mate on their front patio. The smells, sounds, tastes and feelings from these moments are precious memories to me.

I also have distinct memories of some of my final moments with people I have loved before they died. I remember my Opa in the hospital with straws up his nose because he didn't like the smell of his food and had found a silly way to block the smell while simultaneously amusing his grand kids. One of the last days where all my siblings were together involved getting multiple trucks stuck in a mud pit we created in the back field. We drove through it and jumped into it. It was a muddy, joy-filled day. The final conversation I had with my dad on the day he died included him joking around and checking in with me to see how my day was going. I remember the feel of my Opa's hug at my Oma's funeral and the wisdom conveyed when he shared that he wasn't taking any painkillers for the funeral, because he needed to feel the pain of loss that day. The last time I talked to my mom before she went unconscious was skewed by all the pain killers she was on, and yet her spunk and love came through as she joked with me and held me extra long during our final hug. Little, precious moments that may have seemed like regular life at the time, and yet these moments, along with all the other little memories are priceless.

Connecticut also had some lovely lakes and a great boardwalk to walk alongside the ocean. If you had asked me previous to this trip, I would not have listed Connecticut as one of the states that touches the Atlantic Ocean. Then again, I'm pretty sure there's a lot about many of the states I've visited that I had no clue about before. Each has a rich history and stories of its own to tell and have been logged away into my memories. Even the seemingly insignificant moments all come together to make a life.

27

Rhode Island

Next stop: Newport, Rhode Island. Newport is well known for its mansions that were the height of the 'Gilded Age' in the late 1800's, early 1900's. Mark Twain used the term in reference to the thin gold plating that could cover up scores of issues and problems underneath. I toured a couple of the mansions, enjoyed the cliff walk and the beach. As I went to the mansions, what was fascinating to me was all the stories they held. The audio tours were rife with stories, sharing tales of those who owned the house and those who served in the houses.

At one mansion, the audio tour recounted how the lady of the house had a summer party budget, because parties were important in their social society. In today's currency, the equivalency of this budget would be approximately 6 million dollars for summer parties. Reading the stories of the parties was shocking because they went beyond all out. They would have food imported from around the world. Some of the balls were themed and included horses, dogs, elephants and even a dressed-up monkey. I was struck by how easy it would be to get caught up in the social trappings of competition and status and trying to prove one's worth through lavish parties and ornate furnishings and decorations. Even more striking was that while the wealthy 10% of the population lived lavish lives, the other 90% were steeped in poverty and hunger, surrounded by an abundance of food, without money to purchase any.

It's easy to read about their histories and judge them and yet, as humans, we still participate in similar trappings, just in other forms. The family histories of these places amazes me because many of them contributed significantly to society and they left interesting legacies in their stories. My imagination continues to think of all the stories that remain untold. It is such a rich heritage to share our stories with one another. Our stories in themselves become a legacy to treasure and inspire hope and life. It is easy for me to forget this, so being continually reminded helps me remember that my story is important—and that the stories of others, which I carry parts of, are also important to share.

Just as they covered things with gold to make them more appealing, we often try to sugar coat grief. Even in the things we say to each other, we try to fix it or get people to move past it without actually allowing them to sit in it. Grief is raw, painful and hard. There's no getting around this reality. I often had people wish me through grief to the other side, but I was always frustrated with that, because it invalidated my current grief and tried to put an agenda and unhealthy societal expectations on it. Grief stems from the loss of something beloved, so it makes sense that it will be painful. No need to cover it up.

Platitudes are a method we use to try and cover the ugly up and make it more appealing. When sitting with grief, it is often awkward and uncomfortable and we try to fill these spaces with our words, to try and make it comfortable and less awkward. Even though the intent is well meaning, the effect is usually the opposite, because it invalidates the individual's grief and closes the door to them being able to share about their grief. As I have talked to others who have grieved, most of them have stories of unhelpful statements people have made to try and paint over their grief in gilded gold. Even if there are aspects of truth in some of the statements, they are not helpful and the timing is usually wrong.

Some of the platitudes that I've been told or that others have shared with me from their experiences:

"Be strong."

"It was their time."

"This too will pass."
"They're in a better place."
"They're no longer suffering."
"I know exactly how you feel."
"Everything happens for a reason."
"Good thing you have other children."
"I thought you would be over this already."
"A lot of people have been through worse."
"You're young, you can have another child."
"Grief must be teaching you something you needed to learn."
"Let's go do something to distract you from how you're feeling."
"My cat just died, so I know how you feel about losing your mom."
"You've had so much loss in your life, it probably doesn't phase you."
"Everyone loses their parents at some point, so it's not that big of a deal."
"I'm here for you whenever you need me." (And then you never hear from them).

Of course, their intentions are well meaning, but ultimately ignoring and invalidating someone's personal experience is unhelpful and can cause more damage. Better to be silent and fully present with the person. People often want to relate to someone who is grieving, so they share their own stories of loss. Sharing stories of loss is meaningful, but not while trying to comfort someone in the throes of intense grief, because it takes the attention off the person grieving. It is far more meaningful to be fully present to someone and to be willing to sit with them in the hard places of grief. People want to show a grieving person they are seen and understood, so they relate how they understand because they too have experienced grief. Seeing and understanding someone else is best done by listening to them and hearing them rather than projecting your own experiences on the other person. While grief is a familiar experience, it is unique to each individual depending on their situation, so it's vital to take time to listen to their experience of grief rather than assuming we understand how they are feeling, what they are experiencing, or what they might need. Be willing to endure some discomfort and awkwardness. Listen, sit with someone in their silence and in their tears.

It might not seem that significant, but it is no small thing and will have an impact beyond what you can imagine. Just show up.

86

28

Massachusetts

Cape Cod. Martha's Vineyard. Nantucket. Names I have always heard from books, TV shows and movies but I had no idea where they were. Massachusetts wouldn't have been my first guess, but now I have discovered that Massachusetts is more than just a fun (and difficult) state name to say.

I stayed in Cape Cod for a few days. I explored the mainland and took two day trips to Nantucket and Martha's Vineyard via ferry. Cape Cod is beautiful. There are long stretches of beach, soft sand, lighthouses and beautiful landscapes. And it was also the place where my week-long lobster and seafood feast began. Provincetown is at the tip and was the first landing place of immigrants who came over from England. There is a wealth of history and great stretches of national beach to explore.

My trip to Martha's Vineyard was interspersed with downpours, but it was still a great day. Fun fact: Martha's Vineyard has no vineyards (more of a disappointing fact, but surprising nonetheless). It is also where Jaws was filmed. They have a neighbourhood of gingerbread style houses. It started as the Methodist camp back in the day and they would all tent and then they built houses and there's still a meeting place in the middle of it all. It gives a taste of community and times of being together. The island is rife with interesting stories about the history of the island and those who have visited and lived there. I really enjoyed meeting and talking with some ladies that were travelling together. I laughed as they told of the antics of their trip, and I shared about my grieving road trip. We shared about grief and I was thankful for this brief and unexpected connection with strangers. I ended up getting caught in a downpour and returned back to my room that evening soaking wet.

The next day I went to Nantucket. At one point in its history, this was the whaling capital. I visited the whaling museum. There were so many stories and artifacts from that time in history. It made me want to start reading Moby Dick again but then I remembered my previous attempts and decided I would avoid any future attempts.

I enjoy riding bikes, so I decided the best way to see the island would be to rent a bike. The island on my giant map of the US is really small, so naturally, I saw it as feasible to bike most of the island, even though I hadn't biked in years. The guy at the bike shop recommended a few different beaches I could choose between to visit. I thought "why make a choice when I can bike to them all?" How quickly I forget that just because I can do something doesn't mean I should.

Nantucket is beautiful. The beaches are lovely. The bike paths are well laid out and lush with beautiful plants. It was a beautiful, warm sunny day. The old whaling houses were interesting to look at. The lobster in the restaurants was tasty. The lighthouses held history and were fun to look at. There were lakes in the middle of the island with snapping turtles.

However, Nantucket isn't perfect. Some of the beaches have a lot of erosion and garbage strewn in the sand. There are many hills that bike paths go through. In town, you have to ride on bumpy cobblestone streets. Some beaches were foggy and it was cold.

Due to my ambitious bike route that I mapped out in the morning, I ended up riding about 40 kilometres around the island. In flip flops. During the last hour of my ambitious ride, I couldn't even sit on my bike because my butt hurt so much. My flip flops are thin and I could feel my feet digging into the pedals by the end of the day. Did I mention my butt was really sore? Despite all these factors, my day was wonderful. I look at it and laugh at all my mishaps of the day. The mishaps blended with the good and worked to make the day even better. My conversation with myself as I biked around the island all day went something like this:

"I love biking. Biking is the best thing ever. I love the breeze as I ride, I love the freedom as I fly down these hills."

5 seconds later

"I hate biking. Why in the world did I decide to rent a bike today? Why did I rent it for the whole day when I could have just gone out for an hour? My butt is starting to hurt. And this hill will never end."

5 seconds later

"This bike path is just so beautiful. Oooh, look at those pretty flowers over there. And the rolling hills are so wonderful to look at. And it's such a nice day today, I should take my sweatshirt off and enjoy the sun."

5 seconds later

"My butt hurts. The air is getting colder. I should put my sweatshirt back on. Ugh, why did I decide biking was a good idea?"

5 seconds later

"I love biking. This is wonderful. I should do this more often."

5 seconds later

"I can't sit on this bike anymore. Maybe I can bike while standing up? Why did I decide to go to multiple beaches? I think I might be stranded here because there's no way I can make it back up those hills."

5 seconds later

"This is the best! I can use the different speeds on my bike and conquer this island! Maybe I should bike to a fifth beach?"

5 seconds later

"I can't pedal anymore. I hate biking. I'm going to get stranded out here forever and die a slow death. My butt hurts."

5 seconds later

"That was the best day ever! I should rent bikes everywhere!"

You get the picture. Days, moments and lifetimes that are great aren't picture perfect. We tend to only present the positive side of it, but along the way it can also be messy, painful and miserable. Of course, these things don't last forever and everything else you experience along the way makes it worth it. The messy parts are often what enriches it and makes it more meaningful. While the difficult moments suck (I don't want to diminish the pain or anguish of those), they are transformative in who we are and how we engage life if we are willing to face it. I remember my day biking on Nantucket with great joy because I really did enjoy it and I now laugh at the dramatic moments of misery I expressed to myself throughout the day. Had you caught me in one of my more miserable moments while biking, I would have told you that the bike trip was not worth it and I regretted taking the trip. Even so, as I reflect back on this day, the sore butt was worth it. Similarly, entering into the messy and painful parts of life is worth it in the end as we persevere and push forward.

Of course, I also had grace with myself by taking time to sit longer at some beaches and walking my bike back to the bike shop for the last leg of my trip because I couldn't stand to sit on my bike any longer. The agony of my day was blended into the rest of it, contributing to my own growth and strength and rounding out the day in a great way. Life is a mix of many things. Often when I'm in the middle of hard things, I am miserable and want out. When I'm in the trenches of grief, I want to run for the hills. It is hard to be present with grief and much easier to distract ourselves. Moments of great happiness and enjoyment are experienced more deeply in contrast to trenches carved out by grief. The depths of grief bring deeper appreciation of the good and wonderful moments.

29

Maine

Welcome to Maine: The Way Life Should Be.

I glance at the Maine state sign as I drive past. I should stop and take a picture with it. It is my 30th state after all. It feels like it would take too much energy to stop for a photo. I keep driving, noticing my exhaustion. A contented sigh escapes me as I realize I will be here for a few days. Only a few more miles to earn my reprieve from driving.

After more driving, I finally come to the address on my GPS for the Airbnb I've booked for the next few days. I'm finally visiting the other Portland on the east coast. I grab my bag from the trunk and trudge up the two flights of stairs as per the directions for check-in. At the top of the stairs, I punch in the code to unlock the door. The kitchen looks nice and clean, but I keep going to the bedroom where I dispose of my bags, fall onto the bed and fall asleep within minutes.

I wake to the fading light outside. How long have I been asleep? Bleary-eyed, I grab my purse and set out to find something for dinner. The birds are chirping noisily and I breathe deeply. It's good to be outside. The neighbourhood is inundated with trees and beautifully groomed gardens. I walk to the end of the street and spot a store on the corner. Anania's: Your Neighbourhood Store - Italian Sandwiches, Pizza, Pasta. Sounds good enough. With an Italian sandwich in hand, I retrace my steps back to my Airbnb.

I eat my sandwich before retreating back to my bed, with my travel book and computer to do some research and planning for my days in Maine. An endless list is before me. How do I choose? There is so much to do and see here. Portland is filled with fun places to explore, lighthouses and beaches to check out, and a plethora of places to eat lobster (to help perpetuate my lobster eating fest). I jot down some landmarks, waterfront areas and restaurants to check out, forming my rough plan for day 1. There's a national park that's a three hour drive away. That's a lot of driving, but I have a day off of driving tomorrow, so the national park can be day 2, because I really want to see it and I think it's worth the drive. I will have a chill day of exploring on the third day. For my final day, I will go whale watching, because I can't be next to the ocean without whale watching. I book the whale watching trip online, get ready for bed, and crawl under the covers to read for a while. A few lines in, I am jolted awake when my book falls on my face. Laughing, I put the book on the bedside table and turn off the light.

I don't leave my apartment the following day. Hour after hour, I try to coax myself to leave, reminding myself of all the wonderful plans I had made, all the great places I was going to visit. It seems my exhaustion and depression has surfaced. Maine is a lovely state and it is so great to be on the ocean, but maybe I can explore tomorrow instead. The idea of a day to rest with no expectations of things to see and do eases the tension I didn't realize was in my body, and I curl up on the couch with my book and journal.

I glance at my watch. How is it 4PM already? I feel like I've wasted the day. No. This wasn't a waste. I've had a month of driving, visiting people, exploring new places, writing, and processing emotions, all while travelling across an entire country. It makes sense that I'm exhausted and maybe that's okay.

On my second day, I also don't set foot out of the house where I'm staying. I wrestle with myself, going back and forth about whether I should drive to the national park that was a greatly anticipated destination. I decide I won't go. Surprisingly, I don't feel as guilty choosing to do minimal activity today. Yesterday was nice, and I woke up feeling much the same today, so I think I need the rest. My plan for the day: read, take naps, journal, colour, make some makeshift meals from my cooler items, and just take time to be still. I find my familiar spot on the couch, taking in a deep breath, feeling the cool breeze through the window as I look out, watching the leaves blow in the trees, the people walking by, and the clouds floating across the sky. There is so much to do, see and experience here, but this seems like the best thing for me to experience today.

The next morning, the soft morning light awakens me. I notice my body. It doesn't feel as weary. There is an energy surging through me and an excitement for the day to come. I'm going whale watching today. I love whale watching and it's always an activity I enjoy while near the ocean. Anticipation bubbles beneath my skin as I think of the coming day. I wonder what types of whales I will see?

I board the boat, distracted by the smell of the ocean while I try to listen to the safety instructions. The wind picks up, and we are finally moving. While looking out at the waves, I wait for the collective gasp that a whale sighting brings. I hear a cry and look to where the naturalist is pointing, but it doesn't look like a whale. "That's a basking shark." Not a whale, but it's pretty cool to see a shark. Once we start moving again, the naturalist gives a shout. There's a minke whale that surfaces next to us, almost hitting our boat. I'm filled with the thrill of such a close whale sighting.

Morning turns to afternoon, and I enjoy chatting with a few of the other people on the boat. Suddenly I hear the collective gasp, as people on the boat rush to one side pointing out in the water. I spot remnants of a whale blow in the distance as I crane my eyes to find the whale. I smile as I see it in the distance. "That's a black fin whale." I continue watching it and delight in the opportunity to see different types of whales than the ones I have seen back home. On the way back, I am chatting with another passenger on the outside deck when suddenly a giant wave comes over the side of the boat, soaking me and my camera. The day has been so great that I'm not even bothered by being soaking wet. It feels like it's part of the experience.

The next day is spent walking around Portland and exploring. I try potato donuts, which originated in Maine. I choose the savoury ones that are stuffed with cheese and bacon. Delicious. That night I fall asleep feeling rested and content with my mixture of days in Maine.

In the morning when I check out, the AirBnb owner proclaims that she wondered if I was alive for the first couple of days, because she didn't hear a single sound upstairs. I smile, "I needed a couple days of rest after a lot of intense days of travel." While driving away, my thoughts are filled with reflections on my days in Maine.

Rest is good and important. My two down days were a meaningful Sabbath in the middle of my journey where I could rest. The days where I did "nothing" were productive in ways I will never understand. I could just be me and it was enough. I didn't need to do anything, produce something or go and have an amazing experience. Just "being" was good.

It's still funny to me how much I resist rest. I see the continued shift within to give myself permission to not say yes to everything that comes my way. There will always be more to see and do . If I cannot find a place of rest and set healthy and realistic boundaries for myself to live in, I will be worn out and never satisfied. What I have experienced is enough. Of course there is more to see and explore and it's totally okay that I haven't done it all. I can find this place of rest in God, being fully me, enjoying where I am.

In different ways, I also felt overwhelmed and exhausted during the time I spent as a caregiver for my mom. I didn't always take the time to acknowledge my need for rest then either. Sometimes it didn't feel like I was doing much and yet my work was emotionally and physically exhausting in ways I didn't realize at the time. I do not need to feel bad or guilty for needing rest. There have been times since my mom died where I created space for rest that was necessary in my healing journey. Rather than looking back at it with guilt and thoughts of what I "should" have been doing, I can look at it with gratitude, because the rest and space that was created was necessary for me to come to a place of wholeness again. Our lives are full, whether we are working, travelling, parenting or being with others. Rest is important, good and life-giving. Rest is a gift that I am learning to receive.

During my grieving journey, I have also experienced the importance of rest. I often underestimate the toll that life can have on our physical bodies. Sometimes I tell myself I'm only emotionally weary, not realizing that emotional exhaustion also has a physical toll. People who provided respite care for me while I was caregiving were crucial to my survival during really hard seasons. I realize the importance of that respite now and am filled with deep gratitude. Sometimes I felt guilty taking respite or time off but more often that not, that became my life source. I no longer feel guilty about taking rest, but I recognize that it is essential to my survival. I was now recharged and ready for the rest of my journey.

30

New Hampshire & Vermont

New Hampshire and Vermont were the forgotten states. While travelling, I wrote a blog post for each state that I visited, and somehow I neglected to post about both New Hampshire and Vermont until a few days later. My drive through both states was uneventful, but pleasant with picturesque stops. Funny how something can be part of the journey and yet we readily forget about it.

When I lived in Quebec, I visited New Hampshire and Vermont a few times and consequently I wasn't overly excited about these states, because there isn't a whole lot that stands out about them. However, I drove through areas I had never been through (and didn't even know existed) and was overwhelmed by the lushness and beauty of the trees. Seeing the trees had me picturing how vibrant it must be in the Fall when the leaves change colour. I drove through the White Mountains in New Hampshire. You couldn't see them in their entirety as it was a foggy, rainy day, but the fogginess, as always, added to the mystery and wonder of my visit. Being back in the coolness of a rainy day was a nice reprieve after the heat and humidity of the southern states.

I didn't see anything overly spectacular on this part of my journey (possibly why I even forgot about it), but I took in the beauty and enjoyed it. I had seen this type of scenery before and taken walks along similar lakes, but it was an important day. Driving through was a transition to my Canadian interlude, to a place of rest from being on the road. Despite feeling ordinary, it still felt like a special and significant part of the journey. I realize this is a lot like life… our days are often monotonous and much like the others that have come before them. Yet, as we are present to notice and take in each moment, it is special and significant, even if we don't remember it later on.

I often think about loved ones who have died and I hate not being able to remember all my moments with them. There was a lifetime of memories made, and yet so many of them have escaped my memory. Many memories are clung to solely by the pictures I have from those moments. Remembering is good, but I have to remind myself that not remembering all the specifics doesn't diminish the relationships I had or make them less significant, or mean that I have forgotten that person. I remember the essence of those relationships, what they were like and how I felt when I was with them. Although I may not always be able to list specifics of memories, I can remember how I felt, how I was changed by the relationship, and how it makes me feel each day.

There are a lot of aspects of my journey of caregiving for my mom that don't stand out in my memory. There were really hard days, really great days and then all the days in between that seemed to pass by without me noticing their significance. There are moments when I remember a specific time we were together and take joy in the little things of that memory. I rejoice in the incremental, seemingly insignificant moments because their culmination is a beautiful and important part of the journey. So, Vermont and New Hampshire were not write offs but were important parts in the whole of my journey. And perhaps someday I will plan a return trip there in the Fall to enjoy the leaves.

31

Canadian Interlude

I dipped into Canada for a few days of my trip. I had to go to Montreal to attend a training for a summer class I was taking and while I was there I took a couple days to visit dear friends who I used to live and work with when I lived in Quebec. Although this seemed a diversion from visiting the States, I honestly don't know if I would have been able to finish my trip well without my Canadian interlude. Quebec is a second home for me and has a dear place in my life and heart. Consequently, being there was a form of respite in the midst of my journey.

Have you ever experienced deep stirrings when you've visited a place you love? Every time I enter Quebec, I have butterflies in my stomach. Butterflies of expectation, excitement, memories and an anticipation of settling into a place that has been such a significant part of my life.

Quebec carries many memories and holds deep meaning for me. I first moved there when I was 18 as a student to attend Bible School. In the two years before I moved there, my brother and dad had both died and I had graduated from high school. I didn't know how to grieve or that it was okay to grieve and so I had a lot of compounded pain and grief and I didn't know what to do with it. I told myself that if I trusted God fully, then I shouldn't feel pain, not realizing that I was building a wall between God and I by not acknowledging how I was feeling. I used to see my move to Quebec as "running away" from having to grieve, but now I recognize that I didn't know what else to do and felt lost and entrenched in pain that I didn't know how to sort through. Moving to Quebec was an act of survival and fighting for life when I didn't have all the tools or the capacity to be at home in order to face the pain and loss that had built up over time.

Quebec was a place where God started softening my heart and providing me a safe place to start grieving slowly. The figurative walls I had built up around my heart started being removed there, brick by brick. This became the impetus to return to BC two years later to do the hard work of wading through layers of grief and learning how to identify and feel the pain. It was hard work but God initiated the healing process in my heart. When I moved back to BC, I went to university and studied psychology, which provided a safe space to continue grieving and healing.

After graduating from university and working for a while, I decided to move back to Quebec. I had visited many times in the years in between and still had a deep love for the place and the people there. It was a really difficult choice to move there. I decided I would start by working at the Bible School I had attended and then after a few years I would find a more permanent home and job in Quebec.

After two years of working there, I was driving home after a day in Montreal and unexpectedly started weeping. I had no idea why, and a prayer rose out of me, asking God what was happening. I felt like I was fighting God, but I didn't know why. I was filled with a deep sense of foreboding. A week later, I got the call from my mom that she had cancer. It seemed my day of weeping the week before had been preparation for hearing this devastating news. It made sense to move back to BC to be my mom's caregiver. However, leaving Quebec brought a new layer of grief. I had finally started settling into life in Quebec, and leaving tore me from the community there and the life I had been building. My time in Quebec had a lot of challenges, but now I was brought back to BC, faced with an even harder situation.

I have really great memories with my mom in Quebec too. We had a lot of fun visits together exploring different areas. She came out to visit me a few different times and I cherish the memories from those trips together. I have memories of enjoying Montreal's culinary delights together, from Schwartz's smoked meat sandwiches and poutine in Montreal to chocolate dipped ice cream cones at Chocolat Favoris in Quebec City. It always makes me laugh when I think of the time we went shopping in Montreal. We needed new suitcases, and once we had purchased them, we cleverly used them as our shopping bags, filling them with our newly acquired treasures. Whenever we faced judgment from a shopkeeper, we would walk out and carry on to the next store instead. I loved being able to show my mom all my favourite spots in the city and to also explore new spots together. So, whenever I enter Quebec, a flood of all these thoughts and more comes over me.

My time with friends during my 'Canadian Interlude' was renewing and refreshing, especially after 10 days of travelling by myself. Being back in my second home brought up reflections concerning where or what our true home is. My life has been quite transient, and, as a result, my mom was my core definition of home, because no matter where I was or what I was doing, I could always come home to her and she was my constant in the midst of life. I don't have this sense of home anymore. I have a physical home where I live, but it's not the same.

I'm learning that where I am is home. I can be fully present to where I am and who I am with. As Paul says in the book of Acts in the Bible, it is in Christ that I live, move and have my being. As I am fully present to each moment, I can fully rest in God, recognizing that God is my home, even in the midst of uncertainties and when it doesn't feel like I have a constant place to land. God is my refuge. God is my place of rest. God is my constant. God is my home. I still feel an ache at times of loved ones who were part of my definition of home, but I am grateful for the ways in which I can continue to grow in the knowledge and experience of God as my home, and therefore, wherever I am, I am home.

When I was training in Montreal for a few days, there was a labyrinth that I walked each day. I appreciate labyrinths for many reasons and love that it is a physical embodiment of centering myself. It has become a meaningful practice of prayer and being with God. This labyrinth had a "shortcut" to the middle. When you first entered the labyrinth, there was a little sign next to it saying "no!". I laughed to myself that I could just cheat and go straight to the middle. What a great parallel in my life. Along this journey I am on, I often want to be in the middle of the labyrinth (aka the end result). I want to know what the middle is. And yet I am stuck on these other paths, trusting and hoping, that in following the path, I will eventually end up in the middle. In a labyrinth, it is often uncertain when you will get to the middle, because the paths aren't straightforward and they curve in different and unexpected directions. The paths often lead me in the opposite direction from where I think I should be going. And yet, eventually, I end up in the middle.

As I walked the labyrinth each day, I kept hearing God's gentle voice, "be where you are." Generally my response would include asking "But God, where am I going?" "God, when will I get there?" "God, what will it look like?" And over and over again, "Be here. Be where you are."

So far on this trip, I have had this unique experience of being more present to where I am than I have ever experienced. It has been profound and wonderful to be able to enter more fully into each situation and place. I long to live with this type of presence. I continually get caught up with what's next and in doing so, unwittingly fast track what is to be experienced right now. My time in Quebec served as a reminder again to be fully present to each moment and to be where I am. My trip will be over before I know it, so I want to fully enjoy each day until then. The truth of this is so strong and resonates so deeply with me and yet I need to be reminded daily to be where I am.

I am here. God is with me.

32

Pennsylvania

As I head to Pennsylvania, I find myself once again pulling out of the driveway of my home in Quebec. It was four years ago that I last drove down this driveway, realizing that I was now the recipient of a goodbye tradition I had participated in countless times. I drove past the waving hands and smiles of dear friends and co-workers and tried to hold in my tears and save them for the open road. I remember catching sobs in my throat as I turned onto Route 335, leaving behind a place I loved. I was full of confusion and sadness as I drove toward a new and unexpected future back in BC.

When I moved to Quebec seven years ago, it was an exciting time of taking the next step toward a place that had been on my heart since I was 12 and I was finally embarking on what God had been calling me toward for so long. Although I didn't know what my entire future would hold, I knew I would be in Quebec serving in some way for quite some time.

Sometimes our paths take us places we would have never imagined.

I never imagined I would return to BC after only living in Quebec for two years.

I never imagined I would return to BC at all.

I never imagined my mom would have cancer.

I never imagined myself as my mother's primary caregiver.

I never imagined learning about different drugs and medical procedures.

I never imagined spending so much time in the hospital.

I never imagined that my mom would actually die. I thought she would be healed.

I never imagined going to seminary.

I never imagined having no idea what life would entail at 30.

When I first got back to BC, I was trying to be more reflective and prayerful with my photography. It had been a way of connecting deeply with God and allowing the Spirit to speak to me on a deeper level that sometimes only creativity could make room for.

There was a moment when I realized that I was taking a lot of pictures of paths. I kept being drawn to paths wherever I was. Whether it was trails, or railroad tracks or roads, there was something in each one that begged me to take a picture of it. It took me a while to recognize the connection of the photos I had been taking, but as I looked back they spoke to me deeply. They are simple observations and yet felt profound. Some of the thoughts that emerged from my pictures were:

- The path is sometimes hilly, sometimes flat.
- Sometimes I can see where the path goes for miles, sometimes I have no idea what's around the corner.
- The view from the path is at times majestic and breathtaking, other times constricting and ugly.
- Sometimes there are mosquitoes or other bugs. Sometimes there are bears.
- At times the path is beautifully manicured. Other times there are roots to trip over, rocks, or other obstacles.
- Sometimes it's sweltering hot, beautifully sunny with blue skies, or rainy and gray.
- The path can be empty or full of people.
- Sometimes I like to run down it. Other times I need to saunter and pause frequently.

In the end, no matter what path I am on, when I stop and reflect and truly look at it, each contains incredible beauty.

Usually when I am convinced I know the destination, there's a turn in the path to something different and unexpected.

Around each corner, despite my lack of familiarity with the path's layout, destination, or purpose, I can marvel at the journey and trust that although I may not know much about the path, I know the one who has created that path perfectly for me. And I also know that God is faithful and loves me and therefore I can journey with confidence, trusting in a purpose that is far greater than I could have imagined.

I reflect on these things from the middle of my current path. This current road is familiar, but as I approach the border to enter Pennsylvania, it is new and uncharted territory. I went on a road trip through Pennsylvania when I lived in Quebec, but I'm taking a different road this time.

I don't have to worry about all the roads I will be driving today, but rather I can enjoy this road I'm currently on, driving through Pennsylvania, with a stop in Erie. I know that at each point on the road today, as I take the time to stop and look around, reflecting on my surroundings, I will see beauty where I didn't see it, I will know God in a different way and live life a little deeper than before.

33

Ohio

I took one picture yesterday of Lake Erie in Pennsylvania. Today I am surrounded by beautiful landscapes and yet I still don't want to take pictures. It seems I have reached my saturation point. I am excited again about what I am seeing and doing but I feel stuck in a lull where I'm tired and just want to be back home in BC. Grief sometimes feels like this. At times it is an endless road and I just want to be at the end of it.

After a long day of driving, I was entering Cleveland when the sky was suddenly on fire with pink. Looking at the road became a task as I wanted to get lost in this sunset. I had to pull over.

I've reached a saturation point, yes. But God's creation continually pushes me past my saturation point into a position of wonder. There's no way I can take it all in and so I step back to marvel at the God who is reflected all around me.

As I reflected on my own saturation points on this journey, especially feeling it through these states, I realized how we all have saturation points for the grief we walk through and experience in life. I'm thankful for the grace that is extended to us throughout life, especially in the many griefs we face. Grief has repeatedly shown me God's gentleness. I think this is why grief often comes to us like waves, because in the midst of it, there are moments of reprieve, moments of hope and reminders of life. Grief is mixed in with beautiful sunsets and giant lakes that look like oceans, so that in the midst of trying to take it all in and process it, we can both grieve and hope, weep and smile. When we reach our saturation points, we can rest in God who loves us, holds us, comforts us and gives us hope. Grief will not destroy us.

34

Michigan

I wake up on my tear-stained pillow, unable to get out of bed - again. My body, unwilling to move, lies paralyzed. The weight of life, and my inability to engage is a weight on my chest, crushing the air out of my lungs.

I wake up in a hotel room in the middle of the US - I don't even know where I am anymore. This journey has been long - too long. Do I have energy for another day?

An eternity passes until a deep sigh propels me out of bed. Michigan. I'm in Michigan. I glance at the heap on the couch and numbly pull on yesterday's clothes.

I should eat something. Not hungry. I should shower. Too much effort. I should check my messages. Who cares?

I look at the contents strewn in my suitcase. The chaos taunts me. I toss my straggling belongings into the case and slam it shut. Tugging on the zipper, I trap the contents back inside- contained for the day's journey.

I heave my bag into the trunk and climb into the car. Keys. I need those. Where am I going? The map. Follow the map. I turn the keys, waking the engine, shifting into drive, leaving this place.

House. Field. Telephone pole. Car. Gas station. Field. Stop sign. Tree. Fence. Cow. Farm. House. Tree. Field. Lake.

I like lakes. And that's a giant lake. Maybe Lake Michigan? I have never seen it from this side. I pull over.

I should get out. Too much work. I should take a picture. I did that yesterday. I should enjoy this beauty. Why bother?

I press the gas and turn the wheel, my tires crunching gravel as I turn around, heading back to the highway. The endless road beckons me.

House. Field. Telephone pole. Car. Gas station. Field. Stop sign. Tree. Fence. Cow. Farm. House. Tree. Field.

Maybe tomorrow the road will feel different.

35

Indiana

I have now learned that you shouldn't make a travel itinerary based on a song from a musical. People have often asked me how I planned my trip. A lot of it depended on where I had people to visit and stay with, along with specific national parks I wanted to visit. Otherwise I would often look at a state and my potential route through it and pick random cities to stop in or spend the night. Sometimes a city would be familiar because I had heard of it before (in a movie, in a board game, in a book, etc), and so I would appease my curiosity and visit it.

In Indiana, I was excited when I saw the city of Gary on the map. Instantly I started singing the song from Music Man about Gary, Indiana (and yes this song was stuck in my head during much of my time in Indiana). The Music Man takes place in Gary, Indiana and therefore I assumed that meant it would be a lovely place to visit (and would maybe even have a band of children marching through town). Wrong. Fun facts about Gary: the Jackson 5 were born there and that's where they lived. It has also been one of the 10 most dangerous cities in America. Due to great population loss, it has become a ghost town. All the buildings on the main street are boarded up and its desolation echoes on the streets. Driving down the main street at times felt unsafe. I was grieved on many levels as this was yet another side of America to take in and process. Sometimes it feels too overwhelming to hold the sorrow and brokenness of a place and yet our humanity connects us to those places and our own brokenness is reflected there. It is a lot to try to take in and hold.

There have been times when my life and the emotions simmering at the surface have felt like Gary, Indiana. Too often I have pulled over and walked around, determined to stay there for a while. This has come in the form of days steeped in deep sadness where any motivation is zapped up, days veiled over with apathy where I don't care about anything, or also wallowing in self-pity. There is a reality to these moments, but far too often I stay there longer than I ought to, which is to my own detriment. I've learned that in these moments, it is vital to have a support system and to reach out to that support system. This might be in the form of calling a friend, dropping in at someone's house to just be there, or going for a walk. Something to help me reset and remove me from a space that might consume me. I don't want to deny how I feel. I want to notice it, feel it and move forward.

It makes sense now why I couldn't find a decent looking hotel in Gary. Sometimes it's okay to simply drive through a place. You don't always need to spend the night. So, I continued driving through to Chicago.

36

Illinois

I don't like change. I like to plan things and I stick with them. I tend to gravitate toward the familiar because it is what I know and like. This is ironic because I am generally willing and eager to try new things and I don't mind venturing out on my own. While some may see me as adventuresome, I am also fairly cautious and don't like to venture out too much. I will push myself often, but it takes a lot of effort, which usually pays off in the end. Typically though, I need some time to adjust to the idea of something changing if it was pre-planned.

I had originally planned to spend a night in Indiana, but as I thought about it (and realized that Gary wasn't quite as I imagined it to be), I decided that I would rather spend an extra day in Chicago and also see if I could get tickets to the musical, *Hamilton*. Chicago is one of my favourite cities, so why not seize the opportunity to return and walk around, enjoying the sites of the city along with some interesting people watching.

Grief is one of those things that causes upheaval and change in one's life. Sometimes I wonder if my tendency to cling to the familiar and resist change is to maintain some sense of control in life. Grief shows us the areas where we lack control. Loss disrupts the regular rhythm of life. It disrupts emotions. It comes upon us unexpectedly. It is unpredictable, as we never know when it will rear its head and how long it will remain in its intensity. And yet as we allow it to disrupt our days, and attend to it, this paves the way for healing. In moments where I have refused it, it causes more disruption later on. Healing and life flow from our attention to grief.

So, as I mentioned, I did change my plans and although it meant a longer driving day, the result was wonderful. I was able to go see *Hamilton*, a great musical. The man who wrote it, Lin-Manuel Miranda, also wrote one of my favourite musicals, *In The Heights.* This one did not disappoint either - it was fantastic. It's one of those musicals that has so many layers and stays with you for weeks afterwards. An added bonus was that it gave me a good soundtrack to sing along with for part of my trip.

I also visited my friends, Courtney & Nate. I was in Chicago over a year ago for their wedding and it was fun to see them again. We decided to follow up *Hamilton* by seeing *Spamilton*, which was also fantastic, but for different reasons than *Hamilton*. I am thankful for the gift of friendship and memories of seasons of life enjoyed together. And deep dish pizza too, because when in Chicago…

Even though I resist change, I am thankful for it. I don't like my plans being disrupted and yet generally the end result is one that is full of life. The change itself might be painful and the process of dealing with that change difficult, but I am thankful for the opportunities for growth and a deepening of appreciating life in the midst of the hard, wonderful and the mundane.

37

Wisconsin

I'm ready for my day of cheese consumption! Wisconsin is dubbed as "America's Dairy" and, consequently, my Wisconsin plans are simple: consume large quantities of cheese. My first stop is a cheese store. I begin the cheese feast with some cheese curds. I feel like the heaviness of the last few days has been dissipating, but I'm left feeling raw, with a plethora of emotions rising to the surface. As I pull into the second cheese stop, I realize this isn't just about enjoying cheese in America's Dairy, but rather it is me attempting to fill myself so full that I am numb to all the uncomfortable emotions arising. I know I need to feel them and it's important, but I don't want to right now. I just want to enjoy my day. I want a break from the emotions. This break will come in cheese form.

After my third cheese stop, I see a sign on the side of the highway for the Jelly Belly visitor centre. That's a thing? I had no idea this existed in Wisconsin of all places, but it seems like a fitting random road trip stop. And what pairs perfectly with cheese? Jelly beans! Well, I don't know that for sure, but there's only one way to find out.

I walk in and am inundated with bright colours. There are information boards to read about the history of the jelly bean and this company. Who would have thought a jelly bean could hold so much history? In front of me is a sign for the free train ride through the warehouse. I line up amidst the families with children, wondering what a jelly bean train ride will entail.

They hand out Jelly Belly hats as I board the train and sit there as they give the safety announcements. "Please put your hat on as this is a working factory and your head needs to be covered. Keep your arms and legs inside the train, don't stand up, enjoy the ride." Safety briefing complete, the train slowly starts moving.

The conductor recounts some historical facts to us as I notice we are driving through a gallery of Jelly Belly art that has been created throughout the years. My mouth hangs open as I look at a form of art I would have never imagined being a thing. And yet, the artwork is quite stunning in its mosaic of colour, coming together to create images of famous people, iconic paintings and landscapes. Was someone eating jelly beans when they suddenly decided they should probably use the jelly beans to try and create a picture? Maybe they ran out of paint or needed something completely new for their portfolio. People's creativity as seen through art has always been a clear reflection to me of God as Creator. I never imagined this would include art made with jelly beans, but I guess this is out of the box creativity. I can't wait to tell my artist friends about it so they can check out the pictures online. I imagine myself sitting down with a pallet of jelly bean colours. I would likely eat most of the jelly beans needed and would be left with an incomplete picture. Maybe I will stick to hobbies that don't involve consumable art supplies (this cuts out cheese art too, I guess).

Here I am sitting on this train, riding around the Jelly Belly factory, feeling silly in my hat. I am the only adult unaccompanied by children. I am often the only adult by myself, surrounded by families with kids. I'm glad that I choose to do these random things, because they are fun. I don't mind doing things by myself, but there's also a longing for family and to have others to share these random and fun moments with. I'm grateful my family extends much farther than just my biological family, but I feel the pang of loss anew. Grief is a tornado, swirling around my feelings of fun and gratitude.

The train ride ends and we all file off the train into the gift shop. I don't really want anything, and I feel very full of cheese, but I find a shelf of Jelly Belly Belly Flops- misshapen jelly beans that still taste the same, but are discounted because they can't be sold as regular jelly beans. I get into my car, my belly still full of cheese, and I pull into drive. Tears are threatening to leak out, so I open a bag of jelly beans and start inhaling them. I feel sick and I feel numb, but at least I'm not crying. If I max out my physical body, I don't have to feel the surge of emotions screaming silently to be heard.

I feel gross as I drive, now filled to the brim with jelly beans and cheese. There is a tumult of emotion brewing below the surface, but my numbing actions have blocked it from being able to come out, and I feel worse than I did before. I pull over to fill up gas and throw away the rest of my jelly beans and the garbage from my earlier cheese fest. Today I took things that could have been enjoyed and I distorted them, using them in a failed attempt to divert my grief. Why is grief so scary at times? I constantly have the urge to stuff it back down or to numb it with destructive behaviour. This isn't the first, and it probably won't be the last, but hopefully I can recognize what I'm doing even earlier next time and take steps to stop it.

I finally arrive at my hotel for the evening, feeling slightly better physically. I leave my luggage in the room and go for a walk. Back in my room, I grab my journal and sit to write. I pull out a recently discovered poem, 'Autobiography in Five Short Chapters' by Portia Nelson:

I

I walk down the street.
There is a deep hole in the sidewalk
I fall in.
I am lost … I am helpless.
It isn't my fault.
It takes me forever to find a way out.

II

I walk down the same street.
There is a deep hole in the sidewalk
I pretend I don't see it.
I fall in again.
I can't believe I am in the same place

But, it isn't my fault.
It still takes a long time to get out.

III

I walk down the same street.
There is a deep hole in the sidewalk
I see it is there.
I still fall in … it's a habit.
My eyes are open
I know where I am.
It is my fault.
I get out immediately.

IV

I walk down the same street.
There is a deep hole in the sidewalk.
I walk around it.

V

I walk down another street.

Tears form a river over my cheeks as I read these words. If the journey of grief was a sidewalk, my numbing, self-destructive behaviours are the holes in the sidewalk that hinder me from actually feeling my emotions and being honest with myself and others with where I am at. Yet, being stuck in the deep hole contributes more deeply to the pain that is already wrestling to get out. What could walking down another street look like?

I brainstorm: What could walking down another street look like?

- Call a friend
- Journal, naming and expressing my feelings
- Go for a walk, tap dance, or stretch (allowing myself to be in my body)
- Read a poem or book about grief
- Cry
- Write a lament
- Talk to God or sit with God in silence

- Be present in nature
- Listen to music
- Find a creative outlet for my grief (photography, colouring)
- Sit in stillness and pay attention to what's happening internally

I continue to write out some of the emotions that I had bottled up throughout the day. I am filled with hope as I write and feel my emotions. Closing my journal, I am hopeful. I can feel my emotions and the world won't collapse within itself. In fact, I will feel better after. Emotions are okay and perfectly acceptable. They do not make me weak or insufficient. I am grateful for the strategies for the future and how I might respond differently next time.

38

Minnesota

My main regret in Minnesota was not making it to the Spam Museum before it closed. But nonetheless, the drive was still quite lovely and I enjoyed a mixture of torrential downpours, sun and rainbows. I spent hours driving through Minnesota and spent the night there, but I realize I didn't actually see a lot of Minnesota (Spam Museum included). This entire trip I have been reminded of how interesting it is that whatever route I drive becomes my definition of that state. My experience defines the impressions I have of a place. Of course, in talking to others, I am able to better understand the things that make Minnesota what it is. I am grateful for others' perspectives, because my view is quite limited and I will have a skewed view of Minnesota if I rely solely on my experience.

Wisconsin likely has more to it than cheese and jellybeans and yet that was part of my experience there, and I now associate those things with Wisconsin. Minnesota has more than fields, rapidly changing weather, Spam museums and windmills.

Everyone goes through grief. Different stages of life contain different types and layers of grief. It comes in different forms, varying intensities and is experienced in a plethora of ways by each individual depending on who they are and what their life has held. Past loss creates layers with present loss, creating layered grief. I have had different experiences of grief and understand it through my own experiences of loss throughout life. I have also learned a lot about grief by hearing other people's stories that are different from my own.

I continually learn more through listening to varying perspectives. Through these stories I gain a greater understanding of life beyond what my journey has taught me. My impressions and experiences of God are also broadened as I see God as much greater than what I have known and experienced. We can learn together through listening, sharing and sitting with one another through our seasons of grief (and also celebrating and rejoicing with others in those seasons as well).

There are many more roads in Minnesota and in other states that I didn't drive. There are lots of different spots I could have stopped where others have explored. There are experiences I didn't have. There are people I didn't meet. There are stories left untold. I can continue learning and growing as I treasure the moments I have had, listen to the experiences of others and stand in awe and wonder that there is so much more about grief, God, this world, myself, and others that I do not yet know.

39

Iowa & Missouri

Iowa is a state that doesn't get much notice. In conversations with people, I find they often mistake Idaho for Iowa. I didn't see potatoes in Idaho and I also didn't see them in Iowa (then again, I might have, but let's be honest, I wouldn't be able to tell a potato plant apart from… most other plants). There are, however, many cornfields. Most of the corn is for animal consumption but it makes for some beautiful fields in contrast with the sky.

If you want a small town feel, Iowa is a good place to go. I visited friends in Jefferson, Iowa and loved seeing where they lived and enjoyed going to the town swimming pool, golfing and driving through the countryside (okay, the entire state is countryside, but lovely nonetheless). I even came close to hitting a passing train while golfing. It was carrying gigantic windmill arms.

Some of the states I travel through are vastly different from one another, while others blend together in their similarities and landscapes. This part of the trip has contained a lot of driving through the countryside and through small towns. Iowa blended into Missouri as I continued my journey.

I've been to Missouri before, but the area I drove through was different this time. Before this trip, I had visited a friend in St. Louis and had driven there from Chicago. From that drive I learned that there is not a lot outside the major cities except for farmland and small towns. This time, I switched it up, driving through a different part and visiting a friend from school. I have mentioned this before, but it was great to visit people that I went to seminary with for four years and to meet their families and see glimpses of their lives and their places of ministry.

Some days I want to run away and hide from my life. Being in small towns often brings up this longing for me and tricks me into an illusion of thinking I can actually avoid life by moving elsewhere and living a quiet life. As an alternative, I realize I could take steps to build a quieter life at home and make small changes to slow down.

Sometimes my desire to run away and hide happens in the literal sense of going away, and at other times, especially when that's not possible, I "go away" by disengaging and finding various means to mindlessly pass the time. I have a tendency to withdraw. When something appears as a threat or there is uncertainty or confusion, I back off and put up walls and become guarded, trying to protect myself from hurt. If there are emotions that I don't know how to deal with or don't want to deal with, I shut down.

There are so many wonderful things about life and yet sometimes the pain and potential hurt of life seems too much. In a knee-jerk response, I give it all up and struggle to engage.

On the days when I feel weary and done, I am reminded that there is more. On this trip, there are days where I want to be done with the hard work of grief. I want to be done with this trip and engaging continually with so many of these themes.

While not driving in Iowa and Missouri, I spent a lot of time rereading one of my favourite books, 'The Giver', by Lois Lowry. It is a book (and now a movie) about a society that no longer wants to experience pain and suffering and so they create an environment that is free from choice (because if you have choice, you can choose badly and hurt others), an environment where everyone is equal and nobody truly has feelings.

It is a world void of love.
A world void of colour.
A world void of family.
A world void of music.
A world void of dancing.

A world void of death.
A world void of life.

In this black and white world, individuals are assigned jobs, a partner and children. They must follow the rules and use precision of language. It is all very uniform and static. The feeling of love, and even the understanding of the word, are nonexistent.

Jonas is a young man who is selected to become the Receiver of Memory. There is an elder in town (the Giver) who holds all the memories and it is his job to pass the memories onto Jonas. Jonas has only known a world of black and white, with no emotions, and no drastic ups or downs.

As Jonas receives the memories, he starts to see the world in colour. He begins to feel and understand true emotions. He is dazzled by the memory of a beautiful sunset and the experience of snow. He is burdened by memories of war and death. He tries to describe this life to his peers (in the movie) and the conclusion is that there is more.

There is more than the black and white life they have been living.

There is more than the surface, pleasant feelings they have toward one another.

There is a deeper sense of belonging to be had within a family and a home.

There is a great depth that can be experienced within their friendships.

There is incredible beauty to marvel at in awe and wonder.

There is deep joy to be felt to the core of one's being.

There are feelings that move you in ways that words cannot articulate.

There is pain deeper than words can describe.

And in it all, there is life, rich and wonderful, painful, and beautiful.

In speaking of the control that their society has gained, the book says, "We gained control of many things. But we had to let go of others." Cutting out pain was possible, and yet it came at great cost. Jonas recognized the pain, joy and privilege of being alive. At one point, he proclaims, "if you can't feel, what's the point?" Making the choice for fully living was worth it, even with all the harder things that accompany it.

So, when I am tempted to run from pain, hurt, disappointment, miscommunication, confusion, angst, etc., I have to remember that there is more. A life disengaged is not the life that God intended for me, nor is it the life I truly want. Doing the hard work is worth it. This trip and working through these feelings is not a waste.

I still live in a world of colour where there are a plethora of feelings and other things to sort through, but it is so easy to numb all of it and float through.

I'm reminded of the story of the Israelites, in the Bible, right before they enter the Promised Land. What lies before them are giants, fortified cities and many battles to fight in order to live in the land that has been promised to them. There are moments when they want to give up, turn around and go back to Egypt. Back to slavery. Back to oppression. And yet God longs for them to live fully into what God has placed before them. God gives them commandments so that it may go well for them in the land. But they are given a choice.

The choice here seems obvious. Choose life. Choose God. And yet...

There are days when I want to deny any emotions I am feeling and pretend things are all good.

There are days when I want to play games on my phone all day and ignore what I'm feeling.

There are days when I want to avoid interactions with others to avoid getting hurt.

There are days I want to tell myself platitudes rather than wrestle with questions and uncertainty.

There are days when I want to numb and soothe myself with food rather than look at the deeper things happening within.

There are days I wanted to ignore that my mom was dying and cover up the pain.

There are days I want to move to a cottage in the woods and live by myself.

And yet, if (and when) I make these choices, the cost is great. At times my actions, words and avoidance reduce my world to black and white and I miss out. In death, in life, there is more. I need to embrace every facet of life, engaging and walking through each moment, and continue marvelling at the kaleidoscope of colours and the complexities of life.

This is the reality I need to live into today. Every moment. Every day.

There is more. And it's worth it.

40

Kansas & Nebraska

Kansas is flatter than a pancake. Out of all the states, Kansas & Nebraska probably have the worst reputations (or at least that's the sense I got when talking to others about the various states). Everyone in Missouri warned me about Kansas. They talked about how they loved visiting Colorado but the only downside was driving through Kansas. I looked up some stats on Kansas and the topography of the state on average was shown to be flatter than a pancake. I kept thinking about this statistic and picturing a bunch of people measuring a pancake the size of Kansas. I confirmed it—Kansas is pretty flat.

Also, fun fact: Kansas City is actually a city both in Kansas and in Missouri (the bigger area is, in fact, in Missouri). There is a street that divides part of the city—one side of the street lives in Kansas, the other lives in Missouri. Despite the flatness, I found it to be beautiful. I still enjoyed the fields and the views as I drove. That being said, I drove south to north through Kansas rather than east to west, so I think I missed the stretch that might have been most tedious to journey through.

Thankfully, people make a place better, and I had the chance to visit my friend Kyle and his family in Nebraska. Nebraska is also pretty flat. There are lots of fields and you can see the horizon for miles. This raised an interesting question posed by Kyle: if you suddenly woke up from a coma in a hospital room and looked out the window, at that moment, how would you be able to tell if it was a sunset or sunrise? What are the actual differences? After much discussion and "research", we discovered that there is in fact no discernible difference (except for the direction the sun is headed). We looked at a series of sunrise/sunset photos and voted on whether it was a sunrise or sunset and the fact that we were right only about 50% of the time confirmed this. Anyway, I digress…

On the way to the Dakotas, I drove up the eastern side of Nebraska. I had seen a picture someone posted of a cool looking church, so I decided to try to find it. It is called the Holy Family Shrine and is in Gretna, Nebraska. After an hour of driving on random dirt roads and around a few detours, I finally found it and it was stunning. This church is on a hill and is glass. The architecture of it is amazing and the light inside was phenomenal. There's a little stream that goes into the church from the outside and the sound of water added to the serenity of the place. After travelling dirt roads and through endless fields, it was an unexpected sanctuary where I could stop and rest. It was not something I had anticipated seeing in Nebraska, but nonetheless, there it was, waiting to be discovered and enjoyed.

After visiting the Dakotas (see next chapter), I drove back south through the western end of Nebraska and visited my friend Kyle and his family. We spent a lovely day at a nearby lake. Ironically, I wasn't expecting to go to a lake in Nebraska. It's funny the impressions we have of places and that it often stops us from recognizing all the things that are in a place. Nebraska is much more than fields. We also visited the "igloos" near Sydney. There are 801 of them on 19,700 acres and were used for 25 years through 3 wars for storage for ammunition. They were decommissioned in the 60's and now people rent them for their personal storage. It's funny because they are in the middle of nowhere and are a large series of little grassy knolls along the field. This was also not something I expected to see in Nebraska, and had I not been with friends, I would have had no idea what they were.

It would be easy to simply conclude that states like Kansas and Nebraska are merely flat and that's it. I realize that sometimes I simplify life in this way. I do it with my understanding of God, my perceptions of others and my interpretation of my own experience. Grief is not exempt from this. It is easy to reduce my driving route through Kansas and Nebraska to a simple line, forgetting all the complexities of it. My understanding of God through grief and through life might also be simplified to a one sentence statement. However, as you continue to journey, you realize there is so much more depth, complexity, and richness to it all. While Kansas and Nebraska may be flat, they also have a lot of interesting history. They have beautiful sunrises and sunsets. They have stunning big blue skies and different clouds. They have various fields. They have a panoply of different personalities in the people that live there. They have random churches in the middle of fields.

Sometimes I make really strong statements that lead me to places where it is hard to cling to hope and life. I have to continually re-frame and make room for the new things I will discover, for broader perspectives. Life, grief, myself, others and God are far more complex than I could have ever imagined. How amazing it is that we are able to embark on the adventure of discovery and growth as we recognize there is more than we originally thought. Life goes beyond our immediate circumstances. There is more to life than grief, loss and pain, although there are moments when I get stuck there because the pain switches between feeling like a bottomless pit and like suffocating. In these moments I can cling to the hope of more and remind myself that this too shall pass. I'm thankful for each step in the journey that leads me to new places, discovery and healing.

41

North Dakota

There are certain events, without fail, that will trigger grief for me. Even when I think it won't impact me, the emotions that rise to the surface in these moments are still unexpected. One of these things is family get-togethers, especially weddings. My time in North Dakota happened to line up with a family wedding I was invited to.

I have family in North Dakota which seems pretty random but it's an interesting story of when my great grandparents immigrated to North America and were split up from my grandma and great aunt who ended up in Canada while they ended up in the USA. Anyway, my second cousin was getting married and since the timing was able to work, it was great to go celebrate with them, to see family I hadn't seen in a while and meet other family members. It's fun to finally be able to put faces to names that I have heard mentioned over the years. Years ago, on a road trip while moving to Quebec, my mom and I had visited them in North Dakota, and it was good to be back.

Being at a family wedding is bittersweet though, because it makes me miss my mom a lot. This was a wedding my mom and I should have travelled to together. We would have had some crazy travel antics, explored, taken pictures with oversized statues of things (like we did last time) and would have laughed a lot. I'm glad I could go as her representative and yet it would have been so much sweeter to have her join the celebrations. There are moments when I tire of representing my mom in these types of scenarios, but on the flip side, I'm also glad to be able to.

At the rehearsal dinner, my cousin (well, technically first cousin once removed, but I won't bore you with the details of family trees) was telling me that years ago they were with my aunt and my mom at the very same park, hanging out. There was an amusement park next door and he told a story of when they went. That place holds so many memories that I don't even know about and yet here I was, in a place where my mom had been, and enjoyed family. My mom has gone before me in so many ways. I can follow in her footsteps and her legacy of love, family and adventure, without always being aware of it. There were definitely some tears shed in North Dakota, but the trip was worth it and I'm glad I was able to go.

42

South Dakota

How long do I have to sit here? It's an amazing feat that they have carved faces into this mountainside, but how long do you have to stop and look at something to truly appreciate it? Mount Rushmore is iconic. I've heard about it from others and seen lots of pictures of it. And now I've seen it in real life, but I feel bad walking away so soon. I read some of the information and hiked down below to get closer to the sculptures, and now I'm back up at the viewing platform. I have stood up a couple times to go, but have sat back down, because I feel like I should sit here for a longer period of time to actually take it in.

Then again, I've seen the faces, and maybe now I can get back to all the beautiful nature that is in this area. I'm able to sit for extended periods of time while surrounded by nature, but this feels different. It's man-made, but it's fairly interesting. There's also a possibility that I'm overthinking this and I should just enjoy it and then keep going. I travelled here to see this, so I ought to appreciate it, but there is also more to see beyond Mount Rushmore. But also, I've been here awhile and I don't want to sit here anymore, so I should just get up and leave.

I finally get up and begin my walk back to the parking lot, and I am left with many thoughts about how long we need to sit with something for us to truly have been present to it. I don't think there's a straight answer to that but it's something I want to be aware of. I don't merely want to stop somewhere, look at it, take a picture and keep going. This feels fleeting. I want to be able to be fully present to that moment and everything it has for me. I want to pay attention to how I'm feeling. I want to allow myself to feel awe and wonder at the different places I go. As the end of the road trip portion of my trip is drawing near, it is also easier to just keep moving and to not stop and notice. I want to have grace with myself in each moment and I also want to be fully present.

South Dakota has been a good mix of seeing something iconic, enjoying the beautiful scenery and seeing dear friends along the way. After the wedding weekend, as I was getting ready to head to South Dakota, I saw a picture on Instagram posted by friends from Quebec and it appeared as though they were also in South Dakota at that moment (which was unexpected as I had just visited them in Quebec). They were in fact in South Dakota and I was able to meet them for lunch and spend more time with them. I might sound like a broken record, but I am so grateful for the relationships we have in life. I don't know if I can emphasize this enough. I love how God weaves people in and out of our lives. Some are just for a season, some are lifelong and some come in and out in different and unexpected ways and it is wonderful to be able to enjoy each friendship. I have a deep love and appreciation for Andrew & Lisa and their three boys and was so grateful to be able to spend more time with them. I was able to be present in many different ways between the sights and people I encountered in South Dakota.

43

Colorado

It's wild how theology evolves in the background of our lives, shifting incrementally, yet imperceptibly, until one day we are struck with a jolt of realization. We've changed. What we have believed has changed. How we view the world has changed. How we interact, understand and perceive God has changed. I visited a friend of mine in Colorado who I went to Bible School with 14 years ago, and seeing her triggered a flood of memories from my Bible School days, and brought into sharp focus how much grief has changed my theology. As we reminisced and delved into deep conversations, it became apparent how profoundly my experiences with grief have altered my spiritual perspective.

Encountering friends from different chapters of life often serves as a poignant reminder of these shifts. I'm suddenly confronted with a past version of myself, and I see how my earlier beliefs have evolved and expanded. This journey of faith is ever-evolving. The distance between my initial beliefs and my current perspective at times feels like a giant chasm, leading me to question if I've strayed from my foundations of faith. Yet, I realize that this evolution isn't a departure from faith, but rather a deepening of my faith. The challenges and trials I've faced have not only tested, but strengthened my beliefs, reinforcing the foundations of my spirituality.

Some examples of how my theology has changed:

- Trusting God does not mean being "strong" and happy all the time. It means sharing the depths of my grief and pain in raw honesty, recognizing that God can meet me in those spaces.
- The world is not black and white. It is a million shades of gray with so many complexities.
- A lot of my theology is wrong, but the problem is I don't always know which parts are wrong, so I have to hold it loosely. The goal isn't to have all the answers, it's to know God more deeply.
- My understanding of hope has shifted. I clung to it in desperation in moments where I felt like I had nothing.
- Prayer has a lot more silence in it these days.
- Life is really hard. Have grace with yourself and others. You likely have no idea what they're walking through. Be less quick to judge, and more quick to listen.
- Experiencing depression does not reflect a lack of faithfulness or insufficient trust in God.

I imagine my theology will continue to shift throughout life. I am thankful for the foundations that I have in my faith and that I can continue the deepening as I experience more of life, hear the stories of others around me, continue to heal and to experience and know myself and God more deeply.

44

Wyoming

After Colorado I headed to Wyoming. It's funny, because if you're not in the mountains in Colorado, you are in a farm area and it's fairly flat in some parts (at least the parts that brought me to and out of Greeley). In Wyoming I went to Yellowstone National Park. What I wasn't expecting along the way was to go to Grand Teton National Park as well. I am not the best researcher for trips and tend to stumble upon some of the places I end up in, so this was a wonderful surprise.

As I drove into Grand Teton Park, it was sunny with pure blue skies, and I had amazing views. Later on, as I drove through the park, looking back, I noticed the mountains were pretty much completely covered with dark, brooding clouds and you couldn't see a thing. Timing is a funny thing and sometimes it works out in our favour, and sometimes the conditions are much different than initially anticipated.

These stormy moments make me think of grief and how one moment life can be sunny, and in the next moment, dark clouds have rolled in and cloud your vision. Thankfully, these moments of dark clouds aren't as intense or as long as they used to be, but I have to give myself grace for each moment and allow myself to grieve rather than wondering why in the world I'm suddenly in this place. Of all the emotions, grief is the most unpredictable and uncontrollable.

There are moments when I'm reading a book, or watching a movie, when something reminds me of someone and grief shows up through tears pouring down my face. There are moments when I'm driving, and a song suddenly plays that stirs up the ache of loss and grief. There are moments when I look at other people's social media posts with their families, when grief intermingles with happiness for my friends, while simultaneously feeling sadness for the family members I miss. Grief can be triggered by the most random and unexpected things: food, smells, finding an old card or seeing an old picture, playing with my nieces and nephews, walking by a beautiful garden… the list goes on. I am still surprised in the moments when grief arises, especially when it is accompanied with tears. In those moments, I need to feel it, recognize it and then continue. It has become a natural part of the journey that I am no longer resistant to, because it is a deep reality of life and loss.

The black clouds will clear and the storms will pass, but it is easier to experience a downpour if I don't resist it. It's not forever. It is part of living and healing.

45

Montana

Montana was my last state of the lower 48. "How is this road trip almost over?" was my repeated question while driving. It seemed like it had just begun, but it also felt like it had been a lifetime of driving, with nothing else existing beyond me and the open road. I knew the reality that once I returned back home, I would fall back into the regular rhythms of life and this road trip would seem as though it never happened. And yet I felt changed. Each kilometre that I drove felt like continued movement forward, continued healing and continued moments of choosing life.

I met a friend for lunch and then drove to Helena to stay with friends that my mom and I had met years ago on a cruise in the French Polynesian Islands. Otherwise it was a lot more driving, with the knowledge of more driving in my future to get back to BC. I'm cognizant that it would be easy to just throw away these last couple days. I will likely not run into anything new, and I feel slightly desensitized after so many days on the road. But I want to cling to each last beautiful moment of this trip.

I'm brought back to when my Oma and Opa (grandparents) died. They were my dad's parents and died within 7 months of my dad. I had a special relationship with them and loved them dearly, and yet I wasn't fazed by their deaths. It hadn't even been two years since both my brother and my dad had died, and I had not allowed myself to grieve their deaths. I had stuffed down the grief and pain and kept trying to move forward in life. At the point of their deaths, it seemed as though they were simply more deaths to add to the ever increasing list of loved ones who had passed away.

When they died, I didn't have the capacity at that point to grieve the loss. I was desensitized to grief and needed to simply survive and not drown in the waves of grief that were threatening to endlessly pummel me. While growing up, I formed the conviction that if I believed God was good and loved me, then grief was unnecessary and would just be a sign of my lack of trust in God. It was hard to find spaces for grieving and so I stuffed it back down whenever it started to rise. By the time I figured out that grieving was not only acceptable, but an essential part of life, it felt like there was too much to process and I felt ill-equipped. Death and loss had become the new normal I had learned to live with. I downplayed the necessity of grieving and healing.

My built-up grief in many ways felt like a brick wall I was building. Brick by brick, I stacked them until I was protected inside. What I didn't realize was that this "protection" had also cut me off from the world around me and those I loved. I tend toward the all or nothing, so I didn't know how to tackle the mountain of grief that now loomed in front of me, because to face it all at once would have destroyed me. Instead, I experienced God come alongside me to help disassemble the brick wall I had built. We started one brick at a time. Each brick represented a loss and as each brick was removed, my grieving continued and led me toward healing and embracing life.

One brick consisted of me crying in the middle of the woods during a hike, remembering my Opa and missing his presence, wisdom and humour. Another brick involved eating perogies and remembering the perogy feasts my Oma would create with her family lovingly gathered around the table. Some bricks resulted in crying with a friend and sharing memories of my dad and Leon and the things I miss about them.

This grief journey has been lived brick by brick. Some bricks are larger than others, but each is important. In many ways this road I'm driving feels similar in reflecting on all the miles I have travelled. Each mile has looked vastly different and yet each one has been part of this journey. I want to continue strong. I don't want to become desensitized to the last few days of this road trip, or to grief as it continues to be part of my journey. I want to notice, be sad, celebrate and get the most from each moment.

46

Home Stretch

I had planned for my home stretch to take place over three days, but once I found out that my credit card had been compromised, I decided to push through for a really long drive home with a quick stop in Seattle to see a musical. Upon crossing the border, it felt surreal to be back in familiar places while driving home. I got home at 2AM and crawled into bed, thankful to be home safe and excited to leave for my next state in a few days.

47

Alaska

My mom and I went on a lot of cruises together, so it seemed fitting that one of my states should be visited via cruise in honour of her and in memory of our travels. So, after a few days at home, I picked up my friend Anne from the airport and we headed to Vancouver to board a ship that would take us to Alaska. After living out of the trunk of my car for 71 days, it was amazing to unpack and sleep in the same room and bed for seven days straight.

For much of the cruise you could see land. There was lush landscape, beautiful sunsets (I'm sure the sunrises were nice, too, but I didn't get up for those), lots of wildlife (whales, eagles and a Mama Grizzly with her two cubs) and calving glaciers. We had three land stops in Alaska and some cruising through Glacier Bay. In each stop, we did something fun and got to see beautiful new areas. We even went to the Yukon and northern BC one day.

I wouldn't go on a cruise for every trip, but I do love them for a variety of reasons. The main reason is that you get to meet a lot of wonderful people and travel with them for a period of time. This cruise did not disappoint in this area. We had a wonderful group of people at our dinner table each night that we got to know over the course of the week. We were also part of the best trivia team (well, we only won on the final night, but we were the best because we were fun and our team kept growing with new people).

On one of our excursions to the misty fjords, our group stayed outside the entire boat ride (it was freezing and windy at points) and I'm pretty sure we laughed the entire time. There is a special moment of magic that happens in moments like this where you connect with people in a way that allows you to have deep joy, raucous laughter and pure fun. I love that in the midst of life, one of the things we get to experience is those overwhelmingly wonderful moments with others. These are moments that bring a smile to your face when you remember them. Moments that make you chuckle as you look at pictures and videos you took that day. We have all had hard things in life and although we may not know the entirety of one another's stories, we can celebrate life together by living and loving deeply and fully. We celebrate by fully engaging and enjoying one another and our surroundings. These moments are ones that speak deep, unshakeable hope because they point toward God, toward life and meaning.

The boat we were cruising on was the same boat my mom and I had cruised on in our travels. I'm continually struck by the fact that our bodies remember places we've been. It's strange being on a trip where floods of memory come at each turn as you remember previous trips. A lot of these moments on cruises with my mom were also filled with laughter, love, life and celebration and so the remembering brings the mix of sadness and happiness. I'm still learning how to hold those two things together. I often swing from one end to the other and don't know how to express or unpack it for myself. Emotions are overwhelming. And yet as I give myself time to ponder, reflect and remember, I become better at holding them together, of smiling and laughing through the tears and cherishing old memories while creating new ones.

As I enjoy dinner in the dining room, I am reminded of our conversations across the table, our interactions with tablemates and her jokes about trying to steal the silverware. Although I'm not a big bingo player, I always play at least once in memory of my mom, because she would always get so excited about bingo. I think about the chili cooking competition we won once, even though my mom couldn't remember the recipe perfectly, so it ended up being crazy spicy. When I walk by the photo centre, I think about the time my mom had her portrait taken and loved it so much, she bought multiple copies to give to everyone for Christmas, because she figured we should all have a nice picture of her for the fridge or our wallets. There are traces of her everywhere and it makes me feel close to her.

And I have many wonderful people in my life. Those who will travel with me on a whim, those I have met randomly on trips and have kept in touch with. Those who have been friends for years. It's good to have others who hold precious moments and memories alongside me. I'm thankful for those with whom I can weep and laugh, grieve and celebrate and simply be present with. In my writing, I'm also so thankful for all those who journeyed along with me in grief, through my road trip and by reading my writing at present. Thank you for your faithfulness in having journeyed with me. Thank you for cheering me on and affirming me in my journey. Thank you for taking the time to listen. It has been an incredible gift. So many people have been part of this journey in ways they will never know. Although it was sad to see my week in Alaska come to an end, I also know that in future trips, I will continue making memories that will layer on those I already have.

48

Hawaii

Hawaii, the 50th state, the culmination of my three month journey to all 50 states: I have finally arrived. Landing felt a bit surreal knowing that I had completed the journey I had set out on. Hawaii is a pretty great state to end on—lush vegetation, clear blue waters, majestic waterfalls, and pristine sand. It was beautiful and surreal all at once. Driving from the airport to our hotel, I felt giddy being in a place so beautiful and being at the end of my trip.

Choosing when to go on this trip and which island to go to was a difficult decision. In fact, I think I had made plans for about ten different trips before I picked these dates and this island. I settled on the island of Kauai because I had never been there, and out of all of the Hawaiian islands, it was my mom's favourite. It seemed fitting to end my 50 states of grief trip there.

My longtime friend Brooke joined me and it was really special to share this trip with her. I met Brooke when she started dating my brother Leon. He was gracious in letting his little sister become friends with his girlfriend, and after Leon died we remained friends and she has always been a significant part of our family. She came to Kenya and Tanzania on the first family trip we went on after Leon died, we travelled to Cuba together with our moms, and she has always been present for important family moments. She knew Leon and both my parents, and it's nice to be with someone who knows the people you loved who can hold memories with you.

Whenever I used to travel, my mom would always think of the worst possible thing that could happen to me and proceed to tell me to avoid that happening. I knew Brooke was part of the family, especially when my mom wrote in a card, 'Don't get malaria' when she was heading to Grenada. Some of my mom's sage advice also included, "Don't get shot while driving in a convertible" and "Don't get eaten by bears." Brooke and I carry on the tradition of passing along similar life wisdom and warnings. Many days we would make sure to advise one another of what not to do, which turned into peals of laughter. Another quirk we always appreciated about my mom was that she would buy two of everything, one for herself and one to give away (although she usually ended up giving both away because she was incredibly generous). So, when we buy something, we try to buy it in sets of two, in honour of my mom. It is so good and important to have people you can share memories with, whether it includes tears, laughter, or both.

Every day, Brooke and I chose a different area of the island to explore. We enjoyed the beaches, ate tasty food, consumed a lot of shave ice, and relaxed at our hotel. It's a small island and easy to navigate. It is less commercialized than some of the others I have been to and I appreciated that most of the beaches simply had dirt patches where you park under a grove of trees to get there. And there are chickens EVERYWHERE. Before we even got to our hotel, we pulled over at a viewpoint and were suddenly surrounded by chickens milling about. It added to the casual island feel and was fun to see them at every stop. My family had chicken farms growing up, and my mom collected various chicken-themed decor. Being surrounded by chickens felt like an honouring shout out to my mom.

Normally it is a good idea to go to Hawaii when it is cold at home. I considered this idea but I mostly wanted to go and wrap up my trip. So we went in August. As a result, some days were over 40 degrees. I am not a huge fan of heat and so this meant taking it a bit slower and easier in order to avoid getting overheated. For an island that is supposed to get the most rain out of all of them, I think it rained once for an hour during our time there. My mom always told me it rained a lot whenever she would go, but that wasn't the case for us. One of our favourite beaches we visited was in Polihale State Park. It is on a side of the island that is not very inhabited, right next to an army base. True to its description, it is an isolated white sand beach with stunning cliff views on either side. And it was absolutely breathtaking. The sand was incredibly soft. The waters were clear blue. The cliffs stretched along the coast in their green lushness. There were barely any people there and the water provided refreshment from the heat.

We nicknamed the beach Killer Beach. Yes, it was lovely and one of our favourites, but its beauty was not enjoyed without pain. First of all, due to its remote location, you have to drive along a rocky road with potholes for quite a few kilometres. Then you get to the portion where you are driving through very soft and fine sand, wondering if your vehicle will get stuck. But finally, after this treacherous drive, we made it to the beach. The anticipation was high because it was indeed beautiful. Within minutes of walking on the sand, we were dripping in sweat because it was so ho—the kind of heat that drains every ounce of energy you had left to move your legs. I took off my sandals as I do at beaches, but within seconds my feet were on fire. It felt like I would get blisters on the bottom of my feet because the sand was so hot. So I put my sandals back on as I walked toward the water. The sand is so soft though that when you walk on it, you sink in and the sand ends up on top of your sandals, underneath your feet and still manages to burn your feet. And then you reach the reprieve of the water- so refreshing, but the waves are super strong and there are tidal warnings because it's not a great place to swim. But it's beautiful. But it's also Killer Beach.

When we decided to head back to the car, I stood by the water and could see the car in the distance and wondered how in the world I would get there. It felt miserable trudging back through the burning hot sand while dripping in sweat and feeling exhausted. And yet I was still surrounded by such beauty and our laughter at the absurdity of the heat as we trudged back. Well, we did in fact make it back to the car with minimal damage. I look back to our time at Killer Beach with fondness because it was so beautiful. In my head I think "It wasn't that bad, was it?" It was worth it. I see it as quite comical and I do recognize I'm complaining about a trek onto a beach in the middle of paradise, but it was a good reminder for me. We experience a depth of beauty in life as we trudge through the hard and painful stuff. If we are willing to walk through it, there is a richness and deep joy to be experienced that was not there before. This journey of grief has been really hard and it still continues to be at some points. And yet I have a deeper appreciation for the world around me, for people, for children, for the beauty and majesty of God reflected in creation, and for being present to each moment. Grief and pain seem to carve a deeper capacity within to be filled with deep joy, love and gratitude. Just as grief is felt deeply, so the celebration of life can be held deeply.

On another day we took a catamaran to the Na Pali Coast which is only accessible by boat. It was a delightful boat trip. We passed a few different pods of dolphins that swam along our boat, the coastline was absolutely breathtaking and then we had the opportunity to go to a smaller Hawaiian private island and snorkel alongside it. There was a seal in the water with us as we snorkeled. It was a wonderful day. Except for the moment when I was throwing up off the back of the boat as the boat leaped over the waves and we became airborne while clinging to the railing of the boat. Once again though, it was beautiful and I look back on the day with great memories. It reminds me of the times when I was really sick while travelling with my mom. Even now, I don't really remember the sickness, but I know I made the most of it still and enjoyed the different aspects of our adventures. In these moments, I realize it means a bit more grace for myself in slowing down and taking necessary precautions to feel better, but there was still much to be enjoyed.

All in all, Hawaii was lovely and wonderful. We went to Waimea Canyon as well which they call the Grand Canyon of the Pacific Ocean. We became acquainted with the chickens outside of our hotel room, we ate great food (mmm shave ice) and enjoyed downtime and rest in the midst of exploring. This entire 50 states trip has marked a huge transition in my life. It has been a profound experience of exploring and also creating space to feel and continue to process. I believe that God works within us in ways we are not even aware of and I trust that the process of this trip has been transformative for me. I did not always see the transformation taking place and yet as I have completed it, I see where deeper healing has taken place and where there have been shifts in my perspective and understanding. Of course this does not mean life is magically wonderful and perfect but I feel more whole than I have in a long time. I celebrate this and the beginning of a new day and season, knowing that as I continue this next leg of the journey, God loves me and is faithful as he has been all along and will journey ahead of me and with me.

"Yet this I call to mind and therefore I have hope: Because of the Lord's great love, we are not consumed, for his compassions never fail. They are new every morning; great is your faithfulness. I say to myself, The Lord is my portion; therefore I will wait for him. The Lord is good to those whose hope is in him, to the one who seeks him; it is good to wait quietly for the salvation of the Lord." - Lamentations 3:21-26

49

Home Again

My flight home from Hawaii had a layover in Phoenix. Flying home from Phoenix, we unexpectedly flew over the Grand Canyon and Bryce Canyon. It felt surreal knowing I had driven through there a few months before. That was the start of the trip, this was the end. The Grand Canyon looks different close up and yet the bird's eye view gives a completely different perspective that encompasses all the things you didn't see while travelling on the ground. There are a lot of parts I didn't see (and maybe never will) during my 50 states of grief road trip and yet the bird's eye view shows a beautiful journey of grieving, healing and engaging life. Travelling home felt bittersweet on many levels . As I have been slowly settling back into life at home and a new season, my definition of home has shifted.

Today marks two years since my mom died. It is hard to imagine that two years have already passed because my memories and life still feel steeped with her. Yet the last two years have also felt like a gaping hole without her presence in my life. Sometimes when I go to sleep at night, I wish I was again sleeping on the floor next to my mom's hospital bed in the living room, enjoying a late night chat when we both should have been sleeping. When I head to my own home, I wish I was going to hers to sit on the couch next to her. When I'm away from home, I miss sending her texts and calling her to share pictures and stories with her.

In society, there seems to be this pressure that after the one or two year mark of someone's death, you should be "over it". Of course I don't agree with this, but I feel pressured by it nonetheless. Thankfully grieving isn't as constant or as intense as it once was, but there are moments when I am surprised at its intensity and the things that trigger it. Grief is lifelong and although you never know when it might rear its head, the hard days when grief hits become more spread out. Nonetheless, there are moments when I don't want to heal because I would rather just have her back and I resist moving farther away from her memory.

So, as I return home and transition out of a season of intense grieving into a new season, I am reflecting on home. While my mom held home on many levels for me, I can hold her memory in many ways in my own home. My heart aches at times to be in my heavenly home but there is beauty, joy, love and life to be experienced and enjoyed here. I love this quote that a friend gave me before I headed out on my road trip:

"You will never be completely at home again, because part of your heart will always be elsewhere. That is the price you pay for the richness of knowing people in more than one place." - Miriam Adeney

After this trip, I am reminded that my home is scattered across Canada and the USA and other parts of the world with people I love dearly and have been privileged to meet and get to know, even if just for a moment. As I have settled back in at my physical home, I realize more deeply that my friends and family around me hold a piece of home for me in the richness of our relationships and the memories and friendship we share. My brother Leon, my dad, my mom and my grandparents also hold part of my heart and my sense of home even though they have passed from this earth. In all this, I cling to the hope of heaven and life eternal. And my ultimate home rests in God who has always been faithful and present with me, even when I have failed to see it. In each moment, God beckons me and invites me to rest in him, to surrender to my belovedness as his child and to be still.

Home has grown to be so much greater than where I live or where I rest my head at night. Home goes with me wherever I go: it is filled with memories, tears, and laughter. As others carry my stories and I carry theirs, we hold each others' hearts and provide home for one another. I am reminded of the old expression, "Home is where the heart is." This explains why sometimes I feel scattered and fragmented because my heart is in many different places. And yet in recognizing this, life becomes much fuller and richer.

Home is where love abides and where memories are made, held and cherished. Even though my mom is no longer with me, I am thankful she is still part of my 'home' wherever I go. I leave you with one last quote on home:

"Where we love is home – home that our feet may leave, but not our hearts."
-Oliver Wendell Holmes

II

Essays on Grief

50

Choose Life - October 28, 2014

One of my underlying sayings for life is to *choose and celebrate life.*

In doing so, I find it is a positioning of myself toward God to embrace and walk fully into what is before me and to be able to stop in awe and wonder at who God is as reflected in the world around me.

Recently, however, I came to the realization that instead of choosing and celebrating life, I have been waiting for death and positioning myself toward it.

It's been a difficult season sorting through the myriad of emotions that accompany caring for someone with a terminal illness, especially when it is your mom.

When I first moved back to BC last July, my mom's health was going rapidly downhill and there were a couple weekends where she told us this was it, she was ready to go and wanted to say her goodbyes. Every day was filled with the tension of whether or not this would be my last moment with my mom, my last memory. There were moments in the middle of the night where I would peek up from where I was sleeping on the floor and sigh with relief that she was still breathing. Every hug, good-bye or 'I love you' was potentially the last and so I treasured each one. Every action I took was preparation toward her upcoming death. My entire life was on hold as I waited for her to die.

Although she still has terminal cancer, a year and a half has passed and she is doing leaps and bounds better than before. For now she's stable and,

153

despite having bad days, can still do some of the things she loves, like cooking, canning or decorating.

A year and a half later and I am still positioned in a place of waiting for death. I say that with hesitation though, because the reality is that she is dying and I do not want to be ignorant of this fact. But in the process I recognize where I have stopped living in many ways and tried to stop her from living. Hope has been trying to flag me down and I have ignored it.

Christmas has always been something my mom and I treasure deeply. Every year, she transforms our home into a festive wonderland, filling it with themed trees and carefully collected ornaments she's gathered over the years. Last year, when she wasn't well enough to decorate, I did my best, with the help of some incredible friends, to fill her shoes. The trees were lit and dressed, but I knew they were missing the personal touch and love she so effortlessly brings to each one.

This year I returned home from Portland to find the front entrance already glowing with holiday cheer. It was a space I couldn't bring myself to tackle last year—hanging glimmering ornaments from the railings and carefully placing 200 white owls felt overwhelming. But she did it this time. She took the time, found the energy, and made it stunning. It's more than just decorations—the space radiates life, love, and hope.

There have been times where I have tried to stop her from buying new Christmas decorations, because my thinking is 'what's the point?' But daily she teaches me what it means to choose life and embody hope in the face of death. Rather than surrendering to her prognosis, waiting for it to happen, she has been living fully in the unknown. Rather than succumbing to fear, she has loved deeper. She is making the most of every day she has with whatever energy and strength she can muster.

Yes, death is a reality. We need to both embrace it and prepare for it. But a greater reality is the hope we hold onto, and that hope gives us something profound to celebrate. It's a reason to live deeply and meaningfully. It reminds us not to get lost in the shadows of sorrow, but to hold the tension between mourning and joy.

I often find myself stuck in extremes—either clinging to life or bracing for loss—when in truth, life embraces both. The weight of unanswerable questions and my own doubt can be overwhelming. And sometimes, I get so caught up in the fear of losing my mom that I forget the gift of her still being here—the moments we can laugh, talk, and simply be.

There are days I want to shut down and build walls to protect myself, but more and more, I'm realizing: I don't want to miss the beauty that the present still holds.

So every time I see a Christmas tree, I am reminded of choosing life. Of a love that is greater than I can comprehend. Of the hope we have in this life and beyond death. I have said it many times before, and probably will many times in the future, but I will say it again, *L'Chaim – To Life!*

51

Grieving At Christmas - December 23, 2015

Although I have been thinking about writing this post for some time, it has been difficult to form the words that adequately express my thoughts and feelings. My mom died on November 8th, a month ago.

It feels impossible to describe what the past two and half years have held since she began her journey with cancer. Here are a few words that come to mind:

Full of life.
Heart-wrenching.
Memory making.
Sad.
Laughter.
Family trips.
Lunches.
Shopping sprees.
Loss.
Bittersweet.

Of course my list could go on for quite some time, but that is a small window into a season of life that was filled with a richness of joy and a depth of beauty intermingled with sorrow and grief.

All along this journey, I have known my mom would likely die at some point and yet while reality loomed in front of us, it seemed unfathomable that we could actually ever lose her and impossible to imagine what life without her would look like. In many ways, this is why I struggle to properly articulate my thoughts. I am facing a reality that still doesn't seem possible and yet the days continue to pass and life goes on.

I lack understanding concerning the depth of loss and sorrow in this world. In many ways, life itself is a series of losses from the day we are born until the day we die. But losses cannot be viewed in isolation - they represent the countless gifts that have been given. They represent life and transition. And even though my mind cannot always grasp it, hope and life prevail through it all.

As Christmas approaches, countless people keep telling me how hard Christmas is for me this year. Sometimes it's hard for me to be told how I feel or should feel rather than being asked. Christmas has been hard for years. Christmas following the deaths of my brother and dad were excruciating. Each Christmas since has come with a longing for the family who are missing. This year, with over half of my immediate family in heaven, I feel a depth of sadness at what my family has lost and the absence of each one is strongly felt.

When I think about this, it is easy to become overwhelmed with my feelings of grief and my lack of understanding concerning how all of this fits into a bigger picture. And yet I grieve with hope. I grieve with gratitude. And I grieve with the abiding presence of God.

A week and a half ago, I had the opportunity to preach my first sermon. I spoke on Matthew 2:1-12, the story of the magi who come to worship Jesus. This advent I have been reflecting a lot on the magi and why their visit was significant enough to be recorded.

The magi had been waiting and searching for a star. When it appeared, they followed it and it led them to Jerusalem, and then to Bethlehem, where their response was to worship Christ with great joy. Their journey was long and costly and they didn't know where it would lead them. They weren't guaranteed that they would find anything. And yet, with the knowledge and understanding they had, they responded to God's leading, and as a result, encountered Christ.

I have no idea where God is leading me right now. I have no idea why the circumstances of my life are such that they are. I don't see how my life fits into the greater picture of God's plan. Despite all of this, with the knowledge and understanding I have, I can respond to God's invitations in my life. I can turn to God in complete trust and worship. I can trust that despite not knowing how life will continue to unfold, God will be faithful, God will provide, God will direct my path and God will be with me.

So I approach this Christmas with a mixture of sadness and joy. I am holding them together. My mom loved Christmas. Memories of past years remind me of the loss we are now facing, but they also bring me to a place of gratitude and recognition. It is evident that I am living in the legacy and memory of my mom. This is something beautiful to celebrate, acknowledging the incredible gift she has been to me. In moments lacking clarity, I can trust and rest in God and his promises.

In the whirlwind of emotions, in the moments of exhaustion, in the laughter and the tears, I am celebrating and abiding in the truth and hope of Emmanuel this Christmas: God with us.

52

Grieving During Lent - February 10, 2016

This year as the season of Lent begins, I am recognizing its significance anew. I grew up in a tradition where Lent was not highlighted and over the past few years it has become more meaningful.

As the rhythms of the calendar pass by this year, I am viewing them through the lens of being in a season of grieving. Tomorrow is Ash Wednesday, the beginning of the season of Lent, which focuses on prayer, fasting and a simpler life. It is a dark time before Easter.

As I reflect on grief, I see the parallels through Lent.

God takes the ashes of my grief: the moments where things appear grim and hopeless, the feelings of aloneness, the river of tears, the pain that seems bottomless, the ache of longing that is unfulfilled.

God takes these ashes and invites me on a journey of hope. The path that is full of ashes becomes a journey of hope that leads to healing and wholeness. It is a journey of restoration and redemption.

On days when death feels overwhelming, God is summoning me toward life.

On days when the darkness seems to suffocate, God is piercing it with radiant light.

On days that seem entrenched in valleys of sorrow, God is offering me joy.

On days where the loss seems bottomless, God is reminding me of the gift given.

On days when life seems dismal, God is giving me glimpses of hope.

On days when I am filled with fear, God is inviting me to a deeper trust.

On days when I feel lost and adrift, God is welcoming me to find my home in him.

This journey is long and hard. It is excruciatingly painful. Although there are glimpses of the destination, at times it seems far off and unattainable. While it can be tempting to want to rush, the journey is rich with purpose. And if we take the time to be still and notice, God is present. Life, joy, and hope are intermingled with pain. Each step leads to a deeper trust and richer experience of God and life.

Lent may be a regular practice in your life. Or perhaps you have never taken the time to observe Lent. Maybe you are engaging in it for the first time this year. Whatever the case may be, as the days lead up to Easter, may you be mindful of the journey you are on and be intentional about taking moments to stop and notice and to engage God more deeply as you recognize that the journey we are on leads to resurrection life.

53

When God is Silent - October 2, 2016

Since losing my mom, there have been long stretches where I have been unable to write, unable to articulate all the feelings and thoughts swirling around internally. I have been silent.

These thoughts, along with many others, have been mulling around my mind and in my conversations for months now, allowing me time to process and experience the realities of what I have been learning.

In the last year, I have often heard myself proclaim that God is silent.

I have said that I don't hear anything from God because of the silence.

So I took it upon myself to sit with the silence. Rather than trying to fill it with noise and my own words I realized that I too needed to become silent. I needed to listen deeply.

When I took the time to put down my phone, to turn off my music, to breathe deep and be still, to sit and wait, I found that the silence was not so silent.

I have often falsely attributed God's silence to God's absence. Recently, again and again, I am confronted with God's overwhelming and all-encompassing presence. Silence might feel empty, but it's often filled with trust.

In the silence I have discovered a few things:

- Silence speaks beyond what words can.

161

- Silence is loud.
- Silence is full.
- Silence is saying everything.

I love to be outside. Recently I have been spending a lot of time at the ocean. One evening I went to watch the sunset from the beach. I was frustrated with what I had perceived as God's silence. I looked at the ocean and paused. It wasn't saying anything specific and yet as I quieted myself, suddenly the silence around me was saying everything. I could hear the wind blowing through the long grasses. I could see the pink sky reflected in the ripples on the water. I could hear the rocks clinking together as the waves washed over them. I could feel the chill of the cool evening air on my skin. I had to stop and silence myself before I could notice these things and "hear" another way.

In Romans 1:20 it says, "Ever since the creation of the world, God's eternal power and divine nature, invisible though they are, have been understood and seen through the things God has made." God is continually declared and proclaimed in the world around me. God is with me wherever I go. Sometimes words don't cut it. I am continually reminded of this every time I look around at God's creation.

Lately I have realized that perhaps God is so close and God's presence so all-encompassing that I cannot articulate it because it is so strong and overwhelms my senses. In the silence, God sits with me, waits with me, weeps with me, laughs with me, walks with me. God is with me. God's silent presence speaks to God's faithfulness, grace, and loving-kindness.

Throughout Scripture, there is a promise that in seeking God we will find God. At times I have had a very narrow perspective and understanding of what it meant to find God or to hear from God and at times I felt this promise wasn't actually true. In moments when I step outside and step back from my own limited understandings, I realize, as the prophet Isaiah discovered and proclaimed, that as the heavens are higher than the earth, so God's ways are higher than my ways and God's thoughts higher than my thoughts (Isaiah 55:9). God speaks and acts in ways I cannot always decipher or understand. Sometimes God speaks so deeply to my heart that I cannot fully understand or comprehend it but as I sit in the silence with God, I trust that God is fully present and is meeting me.

So, God may be silent, but God is not absent. God is fully present and God's presence "speaks" if I take the time to listen.

I leave you with this quote from Mother Teresa:

> *"In the silence of the heart God speaks. If you face God in prayer and silence, God will speak to you. Then you will know that you are nothing. It is only when you realize your nothingness, your emptiness, that God can fill you with Himself. Souls of prayer are souls of great silence." (from In the Heart of the World: Thoughts, Stories and Prayers)*

54

30 Blankets - October 21, 2016

Letting go really sucks sometimes.

It's hard. It's painful. It's accompanied by tears. It's exhausting. And yet it's also necessary.

Going through a loved one's things after they die is important and a helpful step in grieving, but it's also really difficult.

This past year as I have been going through my mom's things, there is a base recognition that it is all just stuff. And yet, even though it is merely "stuff," my mom took the time to buy these things and made decisions to keep them. They represent things she enjoyed, and aspects of her personality.

The stuff is the physical representation of things my mom had. They are physical things that she touched. How can I simply call it stuff? It represents so much more.

So, getting rid of stuff now becomes part of grieving. Getting rid of stuff is an act of letting go and grieving the loss of someone I loved dearly. It is saying goodbye to the physical things that were connected to her. It's an odd yet painful process.

There are moments where I want to get rid of everything. There are also moments where I want to save everything. There are moments where I bring a lot of things to my house and realize I don't actually need or want to keep it all. And then the more clarifying moments where I recognize it's a balance between the two and it's good to keep some special things in memory of her.

It's a long and arduous process.

So, I now am in possession of 30 blankets (among other things). What do I need with thirty blankets? Easy answer: nothing. And yet cuddling up under one of these blankets on my couch somehow feels like hugging my mom. Of course, it's not the same, but there are emotional attachments that have been built and it is hard to let go.

Yet, letting go is necessary. Painful, yes, but necessary. Otherwise my house would be filled top to bottom with piles of blankets and boxes. Through the process I have become thankful for the physical representation of grieving and how this helps me along the way as I continue to grieve my mom's death.

Since it is far greater than just "stuff", it's important to not take the process lightly. I must also be willing to let go, even though it might be a painful and sad process.

In letting go of stuff, it feels like I'm letting go of pieces of my mom. My mom's life impacted mine in many ways and I'm thankful that her legacy was not at all in her stuff but rather in the impact she had on my life and the lives around her. We are transformed in the time we spend with others and as we share life together. I cling with gratitude to the ways in which my mom's life changed mine. These changes are internal and I could not get rid of them, even if I tried. These changes are with me whenever I travel, whenever I read and write, when I interact with others and host people in my home, when I decorate for Christmas, when I love and play with her grandchildren in the same way she would have, and in a myriad of other ways. In light of these things, suddenly letting go of physical things doesn't seem as hard anymore. I carry her with me.

So perhaps I will only keep a couple blankets and will treasure them because of what they represent. They will be a reminder of who my mom was and the ways she impacted my life. The other blankets, I can share with others, passing on not just an item but a memory and a legacy of love and life.

55

One Year Anniversary - November 8, 2016

November 8, 2016.

Most have been anticipating today as election day.

I have been anticipating November 8 for other reasons.

A year ago I sat beside my mom in the hospital and watched her breathe her last breath.

A year ago my mom's battle with cancer ended.

A year ago began the reality of living life without my mom.

A year ago my friend, travel companion, and go-to person died, leaving a giant void.

This past year has sucked. Of course, there have been some wonderful moments full of life, beauty and hope in the midst of it. But a lot of it has felt like desperately treading water, trying not to drown. It has included a lot of wrestling and processing the different layers of grief that have accompanied my mom's death. There have been attempts to figure out what purpose and meaning looks like and what my days should hold. Most of the year I have felt pretty lost and yet have fought to cling to the truth that I have not been alone and the intensity of grief will eventually lessen as healing continues.

Anticipating November 8, I had a lot of mixed feelings. I have felt the anticipation in my body too. In all anniversaries, my body always seems to know what day is coming, even before I acknowledge it. There are memories of the final special moments spent with my mom. Memories of the last week of her life and the feelings that accompanied that week. Amid feelings of regret, guilt and sadness, there has also been deep gratitude, peace and assurance.

If I'm honest, I think I have had an expectation that after a year I would be able to flip a switch and be ready to fully engage in life again. And yet it isn't so. The sadness still feels incredibly intense some days. The void of not having my mom and not having a solid family foundation still feels gaping. The question continues to loom as to what life will now hold. Sometimes I feel shock regarding the reality that my mom is really gone. There are days when I struggle to choose life and would rather stay in bed all day, hiding from the world. Most days I feel a bit crazy and dysfunctional because I can't seem to get my life together.

In the midst of this, I am quick to forget that I am in a season of mourning and grief. Grief is complicated and messy. Just when I think I'm ready to go, another wave of grief hits, knocking me over again. I put crazy expectations on myself and forget to have grace with myself. My mom and I shared something really special and loved each other deeply. It makes sense that adjusting to her absence in my life is huge. It makes sense that my world has felt turned upside down. It makes sense that there are days I can't stop crying. This is grief. Grief requires space and grace to process and walk through it and heal.

Amid the tumultuous feelings, I am deeply thankful for those who have journeyed with me this year. For those who showed up, called, listened to my memories, shared their memories, cried with me, laughed with me, and have been persistent in asking me how I am truly doing and wanting to care for me. I am grateful to have held my newest niece, who was bursting with life, bringing joy into a difficult season. She was the grandbaby my mom knew about but never got to meet—it is bittersweet, but when I'm with her, I'm bursting with all the love my mom would have had for her. I have felt inadequate as a friend and in different areas of life this year and yet I remind myself of the need to have grace with myself in these things as well. It will not always be so.

And so, a year has passed. A year of mostly hard days and a smattering of days where life felt a bit easier. There have been moments of deep darkness. There have been moments of light piercing through the darkness. There have been moments where I felt like my life would be entrenched in a dark, winter season forever. But I'm now believing that spring does exist and will come. I'm beginning to see signs of spring's arrival. Grief will continue but it won't look the same as it has this past year and it will lessen in its intensity. Life is all around me and in the midst of my sadness, I can continue to fight to embrace life and enter fully in, experiencing deep joy in the midst of each day's panoply of emotions.

I will continue to cling to life and hope as I also work to be honest about my feelings and where I'm at. I'm deeply thankful for the grace that has carried me through this past year and that will continue to lead me toward healing and fullness of life.

56

Haircuts & Transitions - December 30, 2016

Today I went for a haircut.

Why would that be a big deal? It's something people do all the time.

My hair was overdue to be cut. It hadn't been cut for a year and a half. Since August 2015. Since my mom last cut it.

My mom was the one who always cut my hair. Although she begged me relentlessly to go to a hairdresser, I refused. She always said they would do a better job and she wanted to see what they would do with it. But I liked how she cut it. Correction: after she would cut my hair, I would balk about how she ruined it, how I now looked like a boy, how my life was ruined (insert more dramatic comments here) and then two days later I would realize it was the best haircut ever. (She was likely trying to avoid another dramatic roller coaster of emotions from me). I loved the time we spent together in her laundry room with her doing my hair. Why would I go elsewhere?

I would usually sit down for my haircut and she would start cutting and then laugh to herself and say "Oops, I hope you wanted a shorter cut." We would laugh, I would be slightly worried about the end result, but it always turned out great. I treasure each of those memories, each of those haircuts.

So today when I went for my haircut, I was really sad, because I wished so badly that my mom was here to cut my hair. I was nervous, because what if my mom was the only person capable of giving me a haircut I loved? The hairdresser probably wouldn't proclaim "Oops" in the middle of my haircut. Nonetheless, I was also excited because going to a salon for a haircut marked a really important transition in my life, and maybe the haircut would turn out amazing.

A change in my hair length or colour has often marked transitions in my life. Over the last few months I have been noticing a movement towards a new season, a desire to re-engage life again and a deep joy that is blossoming out of the places of darkness I have walked through these past few years.

Today was significant in recognizing that my life is not over because my mom has passed away. I am figuring out what it means to live life without her. A painful yet necessary process. Part of this was finding a salon and booking an appointment. My hair growing in some ways represented an intense mourning period and cutting it has become symbolic of moving toward more acceptance. It represents the hope I have been clinging to that there is newness and goodness in life. And know what? I'm sure my mom would have loved my haircut.

57

Eighteen Years - May 27, 2019

Today marks 18 years since my oldest brother Leon died. After his death, I slammed the door in grief's face. I didn't want to experience the pain it caused. I didn't want to face the reality of my brother's death. I couldn't reconcile what it would mean to grieve and feel deep sadness with the loving, good and faithful God I knew. So I forged ahead, trying to be strong and leaving grief behind, not realizing that I was merely losing parts of myself while dragging around a heavy weight.

The past 18 years have held a lot more grief, great and small. To ignore it is far more detrimental than to pay attention to it. It is imperative to recognize the losses that life has brought; however, it also forces me to look at the many gifts and beauty that life has held.

Sometimes I get sick and tired of grief. It seems to infiltrate so many conversations and memories. It springs up unexpectedly at weird triggers and on anniversary days. And yet, I have to remind myself that it is indeed a lifelong companion and although it looks different as years pass by, it's still there and that's okay. Sometimes I try to ignore it. As anniversary days approach, though, my body and my soul know it and if I don't acknowledge it, I'm left wondering why I'm in a foul mood all day. To acknowledge it and remember involves continued healing and hope.

I still miss Leon even though the deep ache isn't as strong or hollow as it once was. I always wonder what family time would have looked like if he were around. I wonder if he would have had kids and what those nieces and nephews would have been like. I imagine conversations I would have loved to have with him or activities we would have done together. Today I spent the day writing, hiking and swimming in the ocean and remembering Leon. My grief looks so different from the way it did years ago and I'm grateful for opportunities to remember and celebrate and enjoy the world around me with Leon in mind.

58

The Great Sadness - May 7, 2020

Some days it feels impossible to get out of bed. The sun beckons me through the window and I wish I could block it and ignore the day. The weight of life feels too heavy. The routine of life feels too wearying. Eventually I get up, but with a muted feeling that veils the day, dragging a weight that feels too heavy for me to bear.

Depression. It's a big word. It's a word I've avoided for years. I've called it other things, I've tried to ignore it, I've dragged around. And yet when I look back on the ebbs and flows of my life, it brings sense to it.

It took me a long time to utter words admitting my struggle with depression. I was raised to be a strong, independent woman and my understanding of that did not allow room for depression. I saw it as a weakness. I saw it as a failure to overcome something within me.

Being in a pandemic isn't super helpful in this regard. When everyone is invited to group up with their family units, it is a stark reminder that I have no parents, no partner and no children. This has caused grief to resurface with an intensity that I haven't experienced in quite some time.

Dealing with depression has been quite the journey. I have learned to recognize and name it, and to notice when it is skewing my perspectives and reactions to regular life events. I have gone to counselling to keep processing my emotions. I have tried a couple different kinds of antidepressant drugs. I have leaned on friends for support. I have made lists of what to do when

173

depression hits hard. But mostly I have learned to have grace with myself on days that are really bad. I have learned to ask for help and also need to remind myself that it won't always feel like this.

59

Not a Straight Line - November 8, 2022

November 8 is a day that looms on the calendar annually as it approaches. When it arrives, I feel the weight of it. Even if I choose to ignore it, my body knows. Even if there are wonderful things on this day, the sadness is present below the surface, intermingling with the good, inviting me to remember, to pause, and to grieve.

Today marks 7 years since my mom died. On one hand, seven years feels like a lifetime. My "next to normal" consists of me living my life without my mom—not having her to talk to, to travel with, go to shows with, laugh with, to enjoy cooking with… And yet, on the other hand, it still seems like an impossibility that my life could function without my mom in it.

There are moments when my life feels somewhat normal again. And then there are moments when the grief feels so raw that I'm surprised by it. It begs the question: what does healing look like?

I often wonder if there's something wrong with me that grief has indeed become my lifelong companion. Shouldn't we have parted ways by now? It becomes easy to judge my grief journey. It looks different from the person next to me. It is radically different from expectations I had for myself. It often deviates from cultural norms I see surrounding grief. And yet it is my grief journey. It is different from the person next to me. Grief ignores my expectations and it refuses to fit neatly into the false notions about grief from society.

Grief has layers, unexpected triggers, different seasons. It is still a very present reality in my life.

Does this mean I haven't healed? No.

What does it mean to "grieve well" and heal? These are questions I continually ask myself. I have been trying to write this book about grief for a few years now, and I find myself continually hitting a wall, because I feel like I haven't "mastered" grief. Therefore, how can I possibly be writing about it? It's still present in my life and there are moments and days when I still struggle.

Maybe that's what I need to remind myself of. Grief is not something to be conquered. I don't earn a degree at some point that tells me I'm an expert on grief. I'm human, therefore I grieve. I live, therefore I experience loss and pain. Grief has multiple layers and dimensions, and consequently it will hit me at the most unexpected times. It's not about having arrived at a certain point where I have conquered my grief and can "move on" with life. I can keep living life, expecting to experience and move through grief, but I suspect it will always be present on some level. Maybe mastery of grief is the ability to be honest with oneself and others as grief arises - to be able to pause and feel it and then to keep going. Maybe it's not about crushing it, but rather figuring out how to live with it.

There are moments where this might feel discouraging. There are days when it seems overwhelming, because grieving is hard work. It's not something I would choose. But it's not the same every day, every month, or every year, and there is healing that has taken place and continues to take place. There are some days when I really need this reminder. When I look back over my lifetime, I see the ebb and flow of the seasons of grief, the days of differing intensity of grief, and my ability to continue choosing life in the face of grief - all of this is evidence of healing.

Maybe healing looks like continually choosing to engage life, even on the days when I don't feel like it. Maybe it's continuing to invest in relationships, even with the risk of loss. Maybe it's delighting in children playing and joining in the silliness. Maybe grief is celebrating the little things, and the big things, and taking time to remember those we have loved and lost. Grief and healing are in no way linear, and so they are hard to measure, and it is easy to judge ourselves along the way.

So, today I will grieve, because I miss my mom, and because November 8 always brings up a lot of hard and sad memories. But I will also celebrate the healing that has taken place, the growth I've experienced, how grief has shaped me, how my life is different because my mom was a part of it, and the memories and legacy that my mom left behind that live through me. In honour of my mom's memory today, I will eat a really tasty meal, start decorating for Christmas and have a special time of remembering and celebrating with her beloved grandchildren.

So, here's to this journey of grief, in all its crazy back and forth, up and down, zig-zag, and myriad of emotions moments. May we notice grief in the moments when it pops up, may we be gentle with ourselves and may we continue moving forward, continually choosing life on the hard days along with the easy days.

60

How Long is this Good for? - June 7, 2023

My mom was a master of the kitchen. You could tell her that you had 10 friends coming over, and she would have a meal and snacks prepared within the hour. She had a 'Costco Room' in the basement, where she would put all her duplicate pantry supplies, because she never wanted to run out of anything. She had a canning room that had hundreds of jars of jams, jellies, fruit, and meat. She had every spice imaginable, with little labels explaining what the obscure spices could be used for.

My mom's methods of canning were unconventional. I would come home to her canning 50 pounds of red peppers she had roasted on the BBQ. Why? Because they were on sale and she thought it would be fun. Whenever she prepped for canning, the kitchen would be teeming with ingredients, because she had to make 100 jars of everything she canned. It is a mystery to me that when people can food, it doesn't always require massive quantities. In my mind I always thought it was a massive undertaking. I never realized you could just can a few jars if you wanted to.

After she died, one of the hardest things was sorting her kitchen. I had a giant compost bag that I started dumping random ingredients into, because who knows how long it had been in the pantry? But it was hard, and far more jars ended up in my house than in the compost bag. It made sense that I would need 100 extra jars of spices for my house, even though they were years old, eons past their best before dates and had lost their punch of flavour. I piled canning jars of roasted red peppers, red pepper jelly, mystery jam, canned pears and cherries into the trunk of my car. I was able to resist the canned meat though. My dad hunted when I was a child, and my mom had canned sausage that had been made with the meat from his hunting trips. When I realized the meat was over 25 years old, it made it easier to leave behind. After all, how many expired food products can one person keep?

I couldn't throw away the spices, the canning, or the random ingredients for that recipe she had wanted to make one day (despite me having zero interest in making it). These items represented my mom. Each one symbolized a recipe she had wanted to make, or a flavour she wanted to use more of in her cooking. Her ability to cook delicious meals was part of who she was, and if I were to just dump the jars, it would feel like I was getting rid of part of her. I needed those parts of her. I had already lost so much, and, silly as it may seem, getting rid of those 100 jars of spices felt like it would push me over the edge.

So I packed it all up. I brought jars, cans and boxes into my kitchen where there was no space for anything else. Each jar got lost in the clutter of my kitchen cupboards, never to be used by me. Pieces of my grief lay dormant in each grain of spice, in each spoonful of jam, waiting until I was ready to release it.

Eventually I started using some of the ingredients I had hidden away in my cupboards. I blended the 20 jars of roasted red peppers and made enough soup to feed 50 people (perfectly reflecting how my mom would have done it). I put out red pepper jelly next to charcuterie boards at parties I hosted. I generously sprinkled rosemary over my vegetables before roasting them, remembering it as my mom's secret ingredient for roasted veggies. I spread the jam between cookies, when I made my Omi's (my grandma on my mom's side) famous jam jam cookies. I ate canned pears on cottage cheese for breakfast. With each bite I would remember my mom and the way she showed her love to others through cooking. Whenever I shared it with friends, I would proudly proclaim, "My mom made this."

Enough time passed that I realized I was never going to use all these ingredients, and many of them were past their prime. If people did the math after I told them "my mom made this," they may have hesitated to eat my food. Every few months, I would go through my cupboards, and dump a few things. Sometimes it was accompanied with a fervour of organizing and I felt productive and like I was streamlining my cupboards. At other points, I had a deep feeling of sadness and regret as I dumped my mother's labours of love into a compost bag. If anyone had walked in during those moments, they may have wondered why emptying a jar of Italian spices into the compost would bring me to tears, but getting rid of each item felt like I was being more removed from my mom than I had been before. It felt like I was letting go of a piece of her.

I realized this was an odd but vital part of my grieving process. I wasn't able to do it all at once, but gradually as I was able, my physical action of getting rid of an ingredient reflected my internal grieving process.

Tonight I was ready to dump the last six jars of jam. These jars are probably about 15 years old. Maybe they're still good, maybe they're not. Ironically I don't really eat jam regularly, so opening a jar and eating it (and risking that it might not be good anymore), didn't seem worth it. I opened the first jar and smelled it. It smelled like my mom. It smelled like her kitchen in summer as she was cooking the fruit for the jam. It looked like her thick spread of jam she would put on her toast in the morning. I hesitated a moment, wondering if I had made a mistake. There were still five unopened jars. I took two and put them back in the cupboard, realizing I wasn't ready to get rid of all of them quite yet. Their time had not yet come. I opened one jar and realized it was my mom's precious red pepper jelly. The top was dark, but the bottom was red. It was discoloured, which either meant it was old or gone bad, or both. I hesitated. I didn't know I had any red pepper jelly left. Should I put it in the fridge? No. Even as I started dumping it in the sink, I almost stopped halfway through. A tear rolled down my cheek. It wasn't the red pepper jelly I wanted, it was my mom.

61

Who Would I Be? - July 2023

"I wonder who I would have been if you didn't die? I'm also grieving me."

I saw this quote on a friend's Instagram story recently and it's stirred up many thoughts. Part of grieving includes the losses in the future that we will never fully realize. What life decisions would I have made differently? What conversations would we have had, causing me to respond in a new way? How would my social life be different? Who would I have met through you? What opportunities would have come up?

When I think of my brother Leon, who loved to perform, I often wonder if we would have ever done a show together. Maybe he would have taken tap dance classes with me. I imagine my parents and grandparents would have always been the first to buy tickets to any performances I was in. Whenever I'm about to perform, there is a bittersweet feeling. I see other people's parents and family members coming to support them and I deeply wish my parents, grandparents and Leon could watch me perform, cheer me on and celebrate my accomplishments.

It is easy to go down the road of what ifs and missed possibilities and how I might have been different; however, I recognize that the deaths of dearly loved ones have also shifted who I am today and the choices I've made.

Maybe I would have never started taking dance classes. Maybe I wouldn't have returned to musical theatre. Maybe I wouldn't be writing a book. Maybe I would have missed out on other cherished relationships I have.

Although there is grief in imagining different futures with people who have died, I also know that I can't set up camp there, otherwise I will miss what is right in front of me. And what is in front of me is pretty great. I have countless opportunities to do what I love through singing, dancing and acting. I meet new people and perform on stage for live audiences. I get to be transformed as a person through dance and pushing myself as an artist.

As we go into this final week of the Addams Family musical, I am blown away by the love and support of my friends and family. Yes, there are some people missing from the seats in the audience, but there are countless other seats filled with people who deeply love me, are cheering me on and have stood by me and walked with me through the hard and amazing seasons of life. So, thank you to each and every one of you who has ever come to one of my shows. It may seem like a small thing, but it means the world to me.

62

My Grandma's Recipes - September 17, 2023

I come from a family tree of women who made magic in the kitchen. Women who created space in the kitchen that was welcoming and safe for anyone who entered. There is a legacy of recipes and memories from my grandmother's kitchen. From perogies and my Oma making me fruit perogies since I didn't like the cottage cheese ones, to everything Mennonite in between, it was always delicious and you always left more full than you thought possible, with leftovers to take home.

Recently I was sorting through my Oma's recipes. She had them stored in a chocolate-covered macadamia nuts box, one of the dozen she and my Opa would bring back from their trips to Hawaii—it was one of their favourites. The box is filled with hand-written recipes in my Oma's handwriting. Recipes are written on lined paper, scrap paper, envelopes, napkins, the backs of cards and so forth. Whatever paper was in reach was used. There are food splash marks on the recipes, speaking to the love that went into cooking them.

There are side notes, like 'sehr gut' (very good) beside certain modifications my Oma had added. These are recipes filled with love for her kids and grandkids and friends who would come visit. Recipes even include a can of mushroom soup with some other ingredients. There are cutouts from old muffin packages and recipes carefully trimmed from the backs of ingredient packs.

I have tried endlessly to replicate these recipes. The meals or desserts I have cooked always have a hint of the memory of my grandma's food, and yet it is found lacking. Maybe that's okay. I'm not my Oma or my Omi after all. I also know that they both never wrote the ingredients down properly, and would improvise based on feel and touch as they cooked. As I continue cooking their recipes, I have realized that their secret was to cook with love and welcome and the food will always be delicious.

63

You are My Sunshine - June 21, 2024

In the echoes of my childhood fight to quit dance lessons, I never imagined that the sounds of tap dancing would one day become the anthem of my grief, my healing and my deepest joy.

Growing up I was the youngest of four children, with three older brothers. My brothers all did the same activities, so when the girl finally arrived, my mom would not miss her opportunity to show off the fact that she finally had a girl. She used to tell me stories about how my brothers and she thought I should always wear dresses and they should be pink. I was bald, so my mom made sure to get my ears pierced at 6 months old. And when I was finally old enough, my mom couldn't wait to sign me up for dance. And thus began my very short childhood aspirations toward becoming a dancer.

I took jazz and tap. And I hated it. We were expected to work hard, and maybe I just lacked heart, or attention span, but I never practiced and so I would come back weekly not knowing the dance and would get in trouble or yelled at. I had the meanest dance teacher. She had the craziest hair. It was a ponytail on top of her head that stuck straight up and curved to the side. Much of my dance class was consumed by wondering how in the world she got her hair like that. Was it hairspray? Was it a metal rod she stuck in her hair to make it go straight up? It remains a mystery to this day. She would stand in the corner of the room chain smoking as we danced, tapping her stick against the floor so we would stay in time. In between puffs, she would yell at us, telling us what we were doing wrong and direct us to do better and do differently. A successful dance class included at least one of us bursting into tears at some point.

For our dance shows, we had costumes, perfectly curled hair and endless layers of makeup. I wasn't the tiniest girl, so squeezing into those costumes always felt so horrible and did not make me feel good in my body. My mom would wrap curlers in my hair before I went to bed so that I would have perfect curls in the morning. And then there was the makeup. So thick it added layers to my face with a bright red that shone out from my lips. It was always a fight as my mom would try to apply my makeup. And then reapply because of my tears.

My mom supported me, came and cheered me on, dried my tears, but in the end, I think to motivate me to practice, she told me that if I didn't practice, I couldn't take dance anymore, because it was a waste of time and money. Perfect. That's all I needed to hear. Goodbye dance.

I didn't stick with it, and even though my mom had wanted me to dance, I never felt like a disappointment to her. Every night at bedtime she would sing "You are my sunshine." No matter what I did, I would be her sunshine.

Even though I didn't dance or perform, my mom would take us kids to any show that came to town, from concerts, to musicals, plays and dance shows. Questionable shows. I may not have been the dancer she hoped for, but nonetheless she fostered within me a love for the arts. With each show, I would watch and be drawn in, yet left with a deep sense of sadness, because I wanted to do that, but I had quit dance when I was younger. Why did my mom let me quit dance? Didn't she realize that letting me quit was the barrier to me becoming an amazing dancer and performer?

Fast forward to 8 years ago, a year after my mom had died. My mother, my confidante, one of my closest friends, my travel partner, was gone. I thought back to the song she sang for me growing up. "You are my sunshine" had suddenly morphed into a lament. I had been my mom's sunshine, I had made her happy when skies were gray. I never truly knew or understood how much she loved me. The song ends "so please don't take my sunshine away." I wasn't taken away, but the one who called me sunshine was taken away before I could fully understand how much she loved me. Suddenly my skies became completely gray - who would be my sunshine? I had lost the ability to be sunny. I had become a gray sky.

So one day I decided to buy some tap shoes. I always thought about it, how much I loved it and how much my mom loved watching me dance. Before this I had a million excuses as to why I couldn't take tap dance classes.

So I walked into a dance store, and walked out with my new pair of tap shoes. Next step: find somewhere I could wear those tap shoes. Within a couple weeks I had found a studio that had summer tap workshops and they had one for beginners. Perfect.

When I first started, I felt awkward. I felt like I was tripping over my own feet. I couldn't remember the choreography. But I had a much kinder tap teacher. And a deep-seated passion for tap dancing. And inspiration knowing how much my mom would have loved that I was doing this.

With each class it became easier. I was learning to tap dance! The thing I didn't realize at the time was that I was also grieving and healing. There were days that felt overwhelmed with the gray skies of grief and loss where I felt like I couldn't go on. Driving to tap class felt like the most arduous task. But once my shoes were on and my feet started making sounds to the rhythm of music, a little bit of sunshine started reappearing.

Suddenly when I was tapping, life didn't seem so horrible anymore. It felt like I might just be able to enjoy life despite my mom no longer being alive.

Tap dancing became a safe space suspended in time where I could grieve and feel it in my body and transform my grief into something beautiful. It became a place of focus where I suddenly wasn't consumed solely with grief and sadness. It was a place of healing, a reminder of all that is good in life. It became a source of joy and life, paving the way for me to engage life again.

Amid the gray skies, I became sunshine again. And each tap step I took became an honour to the legacy and memory of my mom. I rediscovered the melody of life, and an ode to love lost but never forgotten. Although she never got to see me tap as an adult, I remember my mom every time I lace up my tap shoes, knowing that she would have been my number one cheerleader.

This is a story I wrote for a 'Trespass' storytelling event with Dark Glass Theatre.

The theme was mothers and I had my dance teacher choreograph me a tap dance solo to the song 'You are my Sunshine.' I was able to dance my solo after telling the story and it was a beautiful moment of storytelling and tap dancing.

64

Wedding Dress Shopping - May 10, 2025

I step out of the dressing room to a chorus of oohs and aahs. In the mirror, I catch a glimpse of myself as a bride—surreal and sparkling—surrounded by the bright, beaming faces of my nieces and sisters-in-law. The room erupts with chatter:

"Ooh, this one is my favourite."

"I love this one, but number three still wins."

"Look at the back—those buttons!"

"It's so detailed. It looks amazing on you."

My youngest niece confidently grabs my phone. "I'll take pictures. Don't worry, I've got this. I'm an expert." We laugh as I strike another pose.

I never imagined I'd get to do this—wedding dress shopping. Yet here I am, surrounded by lace and laughter. In the faces of my nieces, I see faint echoes of the woman who raised me.

I keep waiting to hear my mom's voice, to catch her honest, unfiltered opinion: "That one's fine, but it's not *the* one." I miss her honesty—comments I might have reacted to in the moment but cherished later. Instead, I hear her reflected in the voices around me, in the joy and opinions of the girls who carry parts of her. As I head back into the dressing room, their chatter follows, warm and familiar.

That day, the girls were everything—funny, opinionated, encouraging. They picked dresses from the racks, waited patiently, and lit up every time I walked out. Being with them felt like being surrounded by pieces of my mom—her excitement, her enthusiasm, her love.

Yes, there was sadness in that fitting room. But mostly, there was joy. Messy, inherited, unexpected joy—the kind that sneaks up on you and feels like love and contentment.

Standing there in a dress I never thought I'd wear, surrounded by some of the people my mom loved most, I felt a quiet ache rise up beside the joy. This moment wasn't just about the dress. It was about everything it represented: I was engaged. I had found my person. And while it still felt surreal, it also felt right.

I found myself wondering what my parents would have thought of Kelly. I wish they could have seen how naturally he fits into our family.

My dad would have appreciated his calm presence, the way he listens, and always has something thoughtful to say. He'd love that Kelly can talk music and sports with my brothers for hours, sliding seamlessly into their conversations. I imagine them bonding over basketball stories and sports stats.

My mom would have had opinions, no doubt. But I think she'd see what I see: a good man with a kind heart, someone who loves me in a way that feels steady and safe. She would have loved how he is with my nieces and nephews—tender, playful, attentive.

I think of Leon too—how easily he would have welcomed Kelly, how naturally he would have become an uncle to Kelly's kids. He'd probably have a family of his own by now, adding even more love and chaos to the mix.

I imagine the wedding day itself—what it might feel like. Even with all the joy, I know I'll bump up against the absences. There's no version of that day that won't feel, in some ways, incomplete. I'll wear the dress. I'll hold Kelly's hand. And I'll carry, quietly, the weight of who's missing. I'll miss my dad walking me down the aisle. I'll miss planning every last detail with my mom, the way she would've cared deeply about things I barely thought of.

People talk about the glow of engagement, the magic, the excitement. And so much of it *is* magical. There are glittering moments, like trying on dresses with my nieces, or hearing Kelly call me his fiancée. But beneath all that beauty is a soft undercurrent of grief.

It's not that I'm not happy—I am. Overjoyed, even. But I'm also sad. Sad that my parents won't be there to see me become a bride. Sad that my brother won't meet the man I'm going to marry. Sad that my dad won't walk me down the aisle. Sad that my grandparents won't be able to ask him blunt questions. Sad I won't get to call my mom in the middle of planning and argue about centerpieces, only to laugh five minutes later at our ridiculousness.

And yet, amid the sadness, something else holds steady. A quiet truth I keep coming back to: as I expand my family, they are still with me. Not in the way I long for, but in real, undeniable ways. In the nieces who echo my mom's spirit. In the nephews who carry my brother's humor and energy. In their laughter. In the way I love. In the way I'm learning to let myself be loved.

My parents and siblings helped shape how I see the world, how I show up for others, what kind of partner I want to be. They taught me about loyalty, laughter, resilience, and tenderness. They're part of the soil I'm rooted in. And as Kelly and I build something new together, I carry them with me. In every ordinary moment. In every choice. Every day.

I don't know exactly how our wedding day will feel. I imagine there will be tears, some joyful, some aching. But through it all, I'll know this: I am not alone. Love has found its way to me, through the people who show up, who cheer me on, who hold space for all of it.

There will always be empty chairs at the table. But the love they gave me, their impact on my life and personhood, remains ever-present. It shows up in the way I love others, in the relationships I nurture, and in the family I continue to build.

So no, it might not be perfect. But it will be real. Beautiful. Honest. Woven together with sorrow and laughter, stitched tight with hope, and held together, forever, with love.

65

Thresholds - August 22, 2025

Hello! Hello… Hello…

The echo of my voice reverberates through my empty house. It is a sound both familiar and strange, but it feels oddly hollow. This space has held my routines, my laughter, my quiet prayers, my tears, my community—but soon, it will belong to someone else.

I remember the process of designing this home. My brother and I mapped out the space together, focusing on my goal to create a safe space of welcome. Ironically, I moved during the pandemic when the doors of our homes were closed. I waited with longing and excitement.

Once restrictions were lifted, the doors of my home flung open, and so did the possibilities. My vision for this space came fully alive. I muddled cocktails with friends on the back patio as the sun dipped below the horizon, hosted game nights that dissolved into fits of laughter, and lost hours in spirited book club debates. There were midnight heart-to-hearts in the hot tub, stair-fetch marathons with the dog, birthdays brimming with food and friends, puzzle challenges, and craft nights filled with creativity. Friends filled the guest rooms. We tap-danced in the basement. We listened for the whisper of God in spiritual formation circles. I rang in my 40th by fulfilling my dream of having the kitchen island filled with charcuterie.

These years have been more than time passing. They have been brimming with life.

I face this emptiness, a reflection of something stirring inside me, an ache I didn't expect. The quiet rooms, once alive with conversation and friends, now carry the booming echo of my voice. It's a strange kind of silence, not just absence but transition. I walk through these rooms, saying goodbye with every creak of the floor. The grief is layered. I'm grieving the end of a chapter that was centered around this home. It was a container for growth, celebration, connection, and healing. I grieve the ordinary things: the way the house would fill with light at sunrise, the routine of making coffee and slowly sipping it on the couch to start the day. I grieve the extraordinary things, too: the full table during dinner parties, the moments of sacred stillness with others, the spontaneous dance breaks, the unplanned visits that turned into soul-deep conversations.

But maybe what I'm grieving most is not just the physical space—it's the version of me that was shaped here. The woman who learned how to host with joy, who welcomed others while learning to welcome herself, who made room for laughter and grief and everything in between.

This house held all of that. And now, it releases it. And me.

I get ready to create home again, in a new space, this time with my husband and his kids.

Of course, moving is a regular life event that many experience multiple times in life. Unfortunately we don't often name the grief that comes with it. Too often we assume grief belongs only to death. But, truthfully, life is full of losses that don't involve funerals or cemeteries. Jobs end. Routines change. Friendships shift. Communities dissolve. Homes change… Each loss is a small death. These small deaths are not final, but they are real.

Looking back, I can name other "non-death" losses that shaped me. My parents' divorce. Elementary school to high school to university. Friendships that faded over time. Moving to Quebec. Moving back to BC. Each loss taught me that grief is not reserved for tragedy, but often arrives in transitions. Each of those experiences prepared me for this threshold, teaching me that often two things can be true. I can ache for what is behind me while also anticipating what is before me.

As I prepare to move to the island, I feel both the ache of leaving and the anticipation of arriving. My friendships will remain, but they will look different. My community will shift. The routines that once anchored me will no longer be mine.

There is loss in every change. I will miss certain daily rhythms. My friendships will need to stretch across distance. Some people will celebrate with me; others will not. Sometimes the sharpest grief comes when the joy you carry is not shared by those you love. Loss rarely travels alone—it brushes against the losses of others too.

And yet, even with all of that, I sense gain waiting on the other side.

When I lost my mom, I lost my point person—the one who tracked with me, remembered the small details, and carried them in love. I never thought I would find that kind of companionship again.

And yet, in my husband, I have discovered a new version of it. He notices. He cares about the details. He remembers. He knows when something is bothering me. He celebrates with me. We can laugh about our quirks and delight in each other. He is not my mom, and his presence does not replace what was lost. But it has become a new gift—one I never expected. His love has softened the ache of absence, not by erasing it, but by showing me that love can echo in new ways.

Every gain requires a letting go. Marriage brings intimacy, but also the loss of certain kinds of independence. A new home means leaving an old one behind. Even joy carries grief within it.

I am learning to hold this paradox: grief and gratitude are not enemies. They are companions. The presence of one does not cancel out the other. In fact, it may be that the deepest joys are only possible because we have known loss.

Grief is not only about endings. It is also about thresholds—standing in a doorway with one hand holding the door of what was, and the other reaching toward what is to come.

That is where I find myself now. In between. Not fully gone, not fully arrived. It is both unsettling and hopeful. The threshold is a place of ache, but it is also a place of possibility.

To live is to continually engage in the process of weaving together loss and

love, grief and grace, letting go and receiving.
    And this is not the end. It is the doorway.

66

Conclusion

Grief is like the ocean. In a moment, the calm surf can turn into a giant wave that comes out of nowhere, knocking you over. You can shift from swimming forward to feeling like you're drowning. Sometimes the waves seem endless and insurmountable, like the turmoil will never end.

I was nervous about writing this book and hesitant to finish it. I don't feel like a grief expert. I haven't figured it out. Grief feels like something that's always with me, always shifting. What I understand about it one year changes the next. Life is strange that way. It's full of loss, but also of unexpected beauty, and the two are often inexplicably woven together.

Loss comes in so many forms. And if you don't make space to grieve the small things, they accumulate, showing up later in surprising, often unhealthy ways. That's something this journey has taught me—unexpected and expected losses amidst the richness of life.

There were long pauses in writing this book. I held back because I hadn't "fully healed," and I didn't want to feel like an imposter. But, healing isn't a final destination, it's an ongoing journey. Maybe to be human is to carry a few broken pieces inside you forever, and to still find ways to live fully, to laugh, to love. Maybe the presence of grief doesn't mean the absence of healing. Maybe they coexist.

I used to want everything wrapped up neatly with a bow. But I'm learning to live with the messiness, the ache, the unanswered questions. This, too, is part of the journey.

Grief has become a companion, not always welcome, but not always unkind. It reminds me to pay attention. It deepens my capacity for love, for joy, for being present. It helps me live more honestly, more fully.

So, wherever you are on your own road, whether in a season of crashing waves or calm waters, I hope you find grace there. I hope you give yourself permission to feel, to pause, to heal, to keep going.

Grief changes us. But it also opens and expands us. It teaches us to hold beauty and sorrow at the same time, to make room for the full weight of being human. It reminds us that life is fragile and astonishing, that every moment matters. And in that awareness, however painful, grief invites us to live more deeply, to show up more fully, to become more tender, more real. Not because everything will be okay, but because even when it's not, there is still meaning. There is still purpose. There is still life. I will always miss what's been lost throughout life, and especially loved ones who have died. I will always cherish what I've found and the gifts that have been given. Perhaps this is the work and joy of living—to carry the loss and the gift, and to keep choosing love.

67

Acknowledgements

This book was a beast to write - beautiful, brutal, full of tears, laughter, and far too many cups of coffee. It came out of the aching space my mom left behind, and in many ways, she is on every page. Her absence was the catalyst, but her love is the undercurrent. Mom, thank you for teaching me to love fiercely, grieve honestly, and live with my heart wide open. I miss you every day.

To my beta readers - Evy, Jill, Chrystal, Tamara, and Liz—you read early drafts full of raw emotion and typos and still said, "Keep going." Thank you for your encouragement and thoughtful feedback (and for not running away when things got heavy).

Anne, thank you for lending your artistry to the cover - what a joy to have your fingerprints on this project. And Bonnie at Blacksmith Bakery, thank you for keeping me caffeinated and for not judging the number of hours I spent talking to myself at the corner table. Esmay, my faithful fluffball, thank you for your quiet presence, your unflinching loyalty, and for not eating the manuscript.

To the friends who kept asking, "How's the book coming?"—thank you. Your questions kept me accountable and reminded me that people were waiting on the other side of the page. Jackie from the cruise, you rekindled a spark in me when I needed it most. Your words nudged me back into writing, and I'm endlessly grateful.

To all those who hosted me on my grief-fueled, life-affirming road trip: Eric, John, Tara, Terra, Becky, Lisa & Andrew, Matt & Jess, Brett, Erin and fam, Sammy, Devin, Lorri, Nate & Courtney, and Kyle - thank you for the spare beds, shared meals, listening ears, and the comfort of your presence. You gave me places to land.

Monique, thank you for jumping into the trenches of editing and proof-reading. Your eyes caught what mine missed. Carol, thank you for giving me space to tap it out, to move my grief through rhythm and motion - what a gift that was (and still is). Brenda, thank you for providing a safe and honest space where I could process and share my grief. Lynn, thank you for creating a safe space for my tears.

To my husband, Kelly, and the boys, Grayson and Brandon, you joined near the end of this book, but have provided space for me to finish and encouragement along the way. I'm so thankful for this new season with you.

And to my deeply loved nieces and nephews—Parks, Paisley, Stormi, Starlow, Mila, Aiden, and Whitney—you remind me to keep choosing life, even when it's hard. You've taught me more about love, hope, and belly laughs than I ever expected.

If I've forgotten anyone, please chalk it up to the emotional roller coaster of writing about grief—and know I'm grateful for you too. Truly.

About the Author

Vanessa Siemens writes from the deep places where love and loss intertwine. Her writing began as a way to make sense of her own grief and has grown into an invitation for others to feel seen within their own stories of loss. With tenderness and honesty, she seeks to create space for grief to be spoken and held. Vanessa lives on Vancouver Island, where she spends her days with her family and dog, exploring the outdoors, writing, teaching, and companioning others as a spiritual director.

www.ingramcontent.com/pod-product-compliance
Lightning Source LLC
Chambersburg PA
CBHW051448050726
47593CB00005B/1969